Penguin Books

What is to be done abou...

Lynne Segal comes from Aust......, ... psychology at
Middlesex Polytechnic. She is one of the co-authors of *Beyond the
Fragments*, and has been active in the women's movement and
socialist movement since coming to England in 1970. She lives in a
collective household in north London, with her son Zimri.

Mica Nava joined one of the very first women's groups in London in
1969, and has been involved in the women's movement ever since.
She lives in a household of seven people, of whom three are her
teenage sons, and teaches sociology in Cambridge.

Susan Himmelweit teaches economics at the Open University. She is
an active socialist feminist and a former editor of *Feminist Review*
and *Capital and Class*.

Denise Riley is a single parent with two children who lives in
Cambridge. She works as a writer, and, temporarily, as a research
assistant at North London Polytechnic.

Beatrix Campbell is a journalist on the news staff of *City Limits*. She
is co-author of *Sweet Freedom*, and has been active in the women's
movement since 1970.

Wendy Clark is an expatriate New Zealander, and teaches personal
and socialist development programmes in an inner London further
education college. She has been actively involved in gay politics and
the women's movement.

Fran Bennett works in the pensions and social service department
in the General and Municipal Workers' Union. She is active in the
women's movement, particularly on issues of social policy. She has
also written *Your Social Security* (1982).

WHAT IS TO BE DONE ABOUT THE FAMILY?

Edited by Lynne Segal

Penguin Books
in association with The Socialist Society

Penguin Books Ltd, Harmondsworth, Middlesex, England
Penguin Books, 625 Madison Avenue, New York, New York 10022, U.S.A.
Penguin Books Australia Ltd, Ringwood, Victoria, Australia
Penguin Books Canada Ltd, 2801 John Street, Markham, Ontario, Canada L3R 1B4
Penguin Books (N.Z.) Ltd, 182–190 Wairau Road, Auckland 10, New Zealand

First published 1983

Made and printed in Great Britain by
Richard Clay (The Chaucer Press) Ltd, Bungay, Suffolk
Set in Ehrhardt

Contents

7

Acknowledgements

I am immensely grateful to all the members of my household, Chris Whitbread, James Swinson, Steve Skaith and my son Zimri, for their continual and unstinting support, affection and intellectual encouragement throughout the tribulations of writing for and editing this book. As well I would like to thank Elizabeth Wilson, Pat Holland and Neil Middleton for their constructive criticisms; and all the contributors who made the book possible.

LYNNE SEGAL

1

*'The Most Important Thing of All' –
Rethinking the Family: An Overview*

LYNNE SEGAL

'Bringing up a family is the most important thing of all,' says
Margaret Thatcher.[1] And as a woman, she herself can play the
part of the good housekeeper, appealing to those family values
of thrift, hard work and sacrifice. 'It's not impossible to cut
spending. Every housewife with a weekly budget to balance
knows that nothing is impossible, given the will, the character
and the strength of purpose.'[2]

Thatcherism's emphasis on family life, which is always about
women's role in the family, fits neatly with Conservative policies
of tight monetary controls and welfare cuts. But it is women's
sacrifice, their toil and selflessness in the home, which conservative thought must encourage as spending cuts increase
the demands of caring for the young, the elderly, the sick and
disabled. It seems a cynical manoeuvre, but is nevertheless a
powerful one. Stressing the importance of the 'strength of the
family' in these difficult times is powerful because 'the family'
means so much to us. It symbolizes our deepest dreams and
fears. These are dreams of love, intimacy, stability, safety,
security, privacy; fears of abandonment, chaos and failure. It
is a good time to think through again the significance of this
powerful symbol, THE FAMILY.

The family, that pioneering feminist Betty Friedan tells us
today, is essential for human happiness and survival. The feminist movement made a serious mistake when it attacked the
family, reports a recent comprehensive study of marriage and
divorce in the United States.[3] More people than ever are
marrying today. And although many of them – one in three on

present trends in both Britain and the United States – are headed for divorce, many of these will remarry. (Though re-marriages on these same trends have an even higher rate of redivorce.) So marriage and the family appear as popular as ever before, even though we now choose to leave them more rapidly than ever before.

From all sides, it seems, we hear praise of conventional family life. Those 'utopian dreamers' of the 1960s with their intrepid search for new life-styles are much less vocal and visible today, while the scholarly writers from those times, like R. D. Laing, who once exposed conflict, tension and alienation in family life, have mostly revised their views. Even feminists who once located women's oppression in their role in the family, are said to be rethinking their critique. In the United States the pro-family movement, aiming to strengthen men's authority in the family and undermine women's rights and independence, has grown from strength to strength. Some socialists there have even formed a 'Friends of the Family' movement.

But however much former critics of the family may wish to revise their views from earlier more radical times, and reaffirm the family as an institution in this more conservative climate of the 1980s, the conflicts and strains they once explored remain very much with us. Talk of 'the family in crisis' continues to contradict the renewal of confidence in family life. And this is because our traditional family patterns of the last 200 years have definitely changed. Higher divorce rates, fewer births, legal abortion, an increase in teenage pregnancy and the growing visibility of gay and lesbian relationships arouse fears of family breakdown, while the increase in people living alone, single parents, co-habitation and new types of living arrangements, alongside continued maternal employment, all testify to change.

So what has happened to the family? Our traditional family

model of the married heterosexual couple with children – based on a sexual division of labour where the husband as breadwinner provides economic support for his dependent wife and children, while the wife cares for both husband and children – remains central to all *family ideology*. But it no longer corresponds to the typical *household unit*. It never was a perfect fit. But today it hardly seems to fit at all. (For instance, today 56 per cent of married women work outside the home, whereas in the 1920s it was 20 per cent.) Changes in family ideology do not seem to keep pace with other changes in our lives. Can current family ideology therefore obscure the nature of how we live, and the problems we face? In search of an answer, this book will explore changes in the way we live, and their complex relationship to the persistence of traditional family ideology. What is the connection between our actual experience of family life and our image of the family?

Over the past two decades, 'the family' has had a central place in political debate, both radical and conservative – though the focus of that debate has shifted as the issues addressed and solutions posed connect up with newly visible expressions of discontent and revolt from differing social groups. This book will therefore concentrate on those debates of the last two decades, during which, some claim, we have moved from a radical critique of the family to a renewed acceptance of it. We challenge the conventional wisdom which now discounts former anxieties about family life – and dismisses as 'childish optimism' the outlook which once sought to change things – for a neo-conservative realism which opposes even the recognition of change.

My opening article will set the scene for that fierce critique of the family which developed in the 1960s, and the growth of the 'counter-culture' and communal living at the end of that decade. Today moral conservatives like Rhodes Boyson point to that moment of permissive and egalitarian questioning of family

life and sexual values as behind 'all our present ills'. The doubts
of those days and the 'breakdown of parental authority', they
now argue, have created today's disillusioned youth: rioters,
hooligans, muggers and all. This is odd. Those doubts over
family life then were themselves fed by the disillusioned youth
of the late 1950s and early 1960s. Yet that earlier crop of
disaffected youth had emerged from the unquestioning, anti-
hedonistic, status-seeking family of the 1950s, with its values
of thrift, hard work and sacrifice.

Youth, apparently in revolt against their parents' lives and
values, had prompted social scientists to expose and criticize the
family. They described the stifling, inward-looking, stressful
world of the post-war suburban family, with its husbands and
wives, parents and children locked in corrosive conflict. These
critics highlighted the problems of young people attempting to
escape demanding parents, especially demanding over-possessive
mothers with too much investment in their children. Meanwhile, in the counter-culture which developed alongside the
protest movement of the late 1960s, marriage and the family
were seen as sexually repressive authoritarian institutions. 'The
family is a factory for producing submissive people,' the
rediscovered Reich had pronounced.

Missing from the 1960s' critique of the family and sexual
repression was any real awareness or analysis of the male domination integral to existing family arrangements, and to a heterosexuality in which women have been seen as sex objects for
men. Mica Nava, in her article, looks at the emergence of a
feminist critique of the family in the 1970s. Listening to
women's experience of family life, the fast-growing women's
movement learned how women felt isolated, frustrated and
undervalued as housewives and mothers. 'The family in our
society needs to change very rapidly,' wrote Mica Nava back in
1971.[4] Women quickly uncovered the real cost of their dependence on men – widespread depression and breakdown in women

confined at home with young children, frequent marital rape and violence against women and children. Feminists saw that women's private and unpaid domestic work made women vulnerable, economically, emotionally and physically. At the same time, the increasing number of women in waged work found themselves with two jobs. So women began to challenge men's absence from child-care and housework. Mica Nava traces the development of feminist theoretical debate, along diverse routes, making the connection between women's domestic role and our subordination in society generally. She looks critically at early feminist attempts, including her own, to provide alternatives to contemporary family life.

All the articles in this collection are written from a feminist perspective. This means that they look in particular at changes in family life as they bear upon struggles for sexual equality, although, as Nava argues, there is no single feminist perspective. Rather feminism has thrown up fresh approaches to the complexities of family life. For instance, feminists have stressed that the family, even in its ideal form, is not a homogeneous unit. Men, women, children and other dependants occupy different positions of power within it. Feminist writers, alongside other family historians, also stress that our particular family ideal is not unchanging, universal or inevitable. They have traced how wider social structures of production and exchange, and all our social institutions, enter into the 'private' world of the family. So, in at least some of their writing, they have been sensitive to class and race differences in family life, kept hidden by assumed uniformity in family life.

Susan Himmelweit, in her article, looks at the history of the family and its interconnections with the world outside it. She illustrates how a capitalist economy has, in some ways, partially undermined men's traditional power over women in the family, while in other ways it has strengthened gender segregation at 'work' and intensified women's work-load. Developments in capitalism have also exposed the contradictions between home and work, thereby increasing conflict and distance between men and women. The isolation of housework and the alienation of paid work become conflicts felt not only between different family members, but experienced every day within the life of each working woman. The needs of capitalism itself then interfere with the family ideal, partially undermining male authority and separating family members from each other both physically and emotionally, just as its demands for a mobile work-force have broken up wider family and community networks of support and friendship. The inflexible time schedules of our 'working lives' distort our family lives, even without the havoc caused by overtime and shiftwork. When conservative thought blames feminism for undermining traditional family structures, it refuses to see that the strength of the feminist challenge in the 1970s was linked to the weaknesses and contradictions already appearing in that structure.

Despite its contradictions, though, family ideology is not about to crumble. And the strongest support for it in twentieth-century Western thought has been our accepted ideas on child-rearing. In particular, widely popularized interpretations of psychoanalytic thought since the Second World War have stressed the essential mother–child bond, ideally continuous and undisturbed in the early years. 'Young children need full-time mothers,' child psychologists tell us. 'Nature intended mother and child to be together,' pop biologists assure us. Yet the idea of such full-time, private mothering of children is a recent one, uncharacteristic of other times and other places. Feminists have explored the historical and cultural influences behind our conception of motherhood, alongside our ambivalent experiences of it, in the relative isolation of contemporary motherhood, especially during the child's pre-school years.

Denise Riley takes up the question of the needs of children, asking pertinently what are needs, and where do they come from? Though feminists are constantly seen as women against motherhood and children, the women's movement has fought tenaciously for changes which would enable women to have, or not to have, children in conditions of their choice. This has meant campaigns for more nurseries, increased child benefits, shared parenting, better housing and welfare, as well as ones for adequate contraception and abortion facilities. Is there a conflict between the needs of children and women's demands for equality? Many feminists would emphasize instead the conflict between the needs met by women in the family and the values of the market, with 'maternal deprivation' a myth to keep women at home and men excused from child-care.

Denise Riley indicates some of the contradictions of mothering for women, as both a source of conflict and of gratification. Indeed, in our sexist society, home can be the one place women feel any degree of power and control. Mica Nava mentions, though we cannot adequately cover in this collection, more recent feminist debate on the use of psychoanalytic perspectives to understand the internalization of gender roles within the family, and the strength of unconscious mental processes which make change in adult life extremely difficult. In particular, feminists such as Dinnerstein and Chodorow have stressed how women's almost exclusive role in mothering, in the context of overall male authority, is crucial in *creating* deeply-lying sex differences in personality which perpetuate gender inequality.[5] In their view, the maternal role creates a girl's capacity and desire to mother (and hence her continual subordination) and a boy's life-long expectation of female servicing together with his devaluation and fear of women. Only men's shared involvement in infant care, they argue, would begin to undermine this hierarchical gender division. However, Denise Riley ponders some possible limitations to any premature assumptions of 'shared parenting' as the solution to problems of child-care – particularly at a time when the need to struggle for public provision remains, in the face of cuts, more crucial than ever.

Men's devaluation and fear of women is directed particularly at women as active sexual beings. You don't have to be the Ripper to isolate 'whores' from 'innocent' women, the former deserving punishment and the latter needing protection. The Church, the state, the judiciary and every image of popular culture already do that. At first with enthusiasm, and then with increasing difficulty and silence, feminists in the 1970s discussed marriage, sex and the family. Marriage, with its legal obligations, institutionalized male authority and compulsory heterosexuality, was seen as incompatible with passionate love and sexual freedom. It provided the framework for the disastrous madonna/whore duality. So feminists once argued.

Ironically, in current family ideology, marriage has been in-creasingly linked with sexual pleasure. Attitudes to sexuality are thought to have changed dramatically from Victorian times to the present. We have swung, in expert opinion, from the nega-tive attitudes of the Victorians where sex became some sort of dangerous and destructive power, confined, 'fortunately for civilization', mainly to men, to one where sex is now seen as both joyful and creative for men and *especially* for women. Sexologists since the Second World War, scorning the pains of the Freudian libido, came to emphasize the 'Joy of Sex', to which all *should* aspire, *and* without which no marriage is safe, secure or happy. Even feminists absorbed some of the com-mandments of the sexological handbooks to happiness. 'First find your clitoris, and then caress it to orgasm. Teach your partner to do the same.' Men acknowledging the clitoris *was* important to women's heterosexual pleasure, and more accessi-ble contraception and abortion from the late 1960s, was an enormous gain for women.

But there remained a problem which the sexologists obscured. More fundamentally, many traditional sexual attitudes have remained unchanged over the last hundred years. Sexual behaviour, whether seen as threatening or joyful, is still seen as the expression of some sort of powerful, *biological* urge. It is still concealed from children, confined to a very special area of life cut off from others, acceptable only in certain types of relationship. That is, it is still forbidden, still arouses disgust, is still surrounded by taboos, and above all else, despite 'tolerance' towards homosexuality, is still seen essentially in terms of a genital heterosexuality which men initiate and control. The association of male sexuality, masculinity and power, where 'impotence' literally signifies powerlessness, means that male sexuality in our culture *is* threatening to women. Men 'prove' their masculinity through sexual 'conquest' – which so often produces sexual coercion – of women. Marriage may therefore seem the only 'safe' place for female sexuality, just as it may at least in principle provide the only adequate security for women who are pregnant.

Beatrix Campbell looks at the effects of sexual reform and the development of family planning this century in regularizing women's sexuality as mothers *within* marriage. She outlines some of the feminist campaigns around sexual politics and the family, emphasizing the importance of the growth of the Women's Aid Movement in allowing battered women to escape from and challenge men's power in the family. In organizing against the everyday horror of male sexual violence and intimidation, women are challenging the myth, which creates its own reality, of women's need for male 'protection' *from other men*! There has been a split in the women's movement between feminists who see men as the enemy, and those who see sexism and the oppressive elements of masculinity as the problem. This split has contributed to a growing silence on any positive image of heterosexuality, and an understanding of lesbianism more as a political than a sexual practice. Bea Campbell discusses the relationship between lesbianism and heterosexuality in the women's movement, and the need for an alliance which can challenge the sexual ideology of the family. For it is *this ideology* which makes deviants of all whose sexual practice is outside of marriage; which directly threatens lesbian mothers with the loss of their children; and which stands in the way of any adequate understanding of women's sexuality – however it is manifest.

Right up to the 1970s, there remained a crushing social stigma attached to the unmarried mother (which has abated but not disappeared in many social groups today). Women did not *choose* motherhood outside of marriage. The fear and shame of illegitimacy and the 'fallen woman', as evidence of women's illicit sexuality, gave men and not women control of women's sexuality and fertility through the institution of marriage. A challenge to that institution, and hence to men's control over women's sexuality and fertility, has been made by those women who have, over the past two decades, refused to marry to legitimate their sexual lives. Even more importantly, and often with more difficulty in the face of personal pressure and social stigma, certain women were able to take control of their own fertility, by choosing to have children outside of marriage. Women's refusal to marry is not simply a personal choice or question of 'life-style'. It is a crucial *political* choice. Challenging the institution of marriage has meant for feminists not just a refusal to marry, but also establishing an oppositional culture and networks of friendship and support. We have sought ways of meeting our needs for intimacy and security, and for assistance with child-care, outside of the gender divisions and male domination of conventional marriage. Feminists have also rejected family ideology's emphasis on *private* provision for these needs, as well as the selfishness of a structure which essentially cares only for its own.

This has been both hard and exhausting in practice. **Wendy Clark** discusses the pressure of the family ideal on those who live outside of conventional families. She focuses on issues feminists have often avoided. Do collective households really meet the many unseen and unexamined needs we take into them, as we try to build alternative lives and communities beyond biological and legal ties? She reflects on her own experiences of personal relationships inside collectives, where people unconsciously seek to create or else to escape from aspects of their own family histories. It is, she feels, our frequent failure or inability to examine and understand these needs that has destroyed so many of our collective households.

The family ideal and women's domestic role are, of course, supported by the state and its institutions in our society. 'During marriage most women will not be gainfully occupied,' said Beveridge in 1942. History proved him wrong, but to this day the state is turning a blind eye to history. Marriage as an institution of the state places women in legal and financial dependence on men. Legal reforms in marriage over the last century mean that husbands no longer have absolute rights over their wives' children, property and income. But the effects of marital reform and the development of the British Welfare State on women have been contradictory. State intervention in the form of benefits, allowances and expanded welfare services offered some security and assistance to families, making women with children less vulnerable than ever before. But state policies also strengthened existing gender divisions and women's dependency by assuming in every marriage a male breadwinner providing for the wife and children.

Fran Bennett outlines the complex relationship between state policies and women's dependence. In the early 1970s, the re-emerging women's movement related to the state as primarily coercive, denying, begrudging and threatening towards single mothers, claimants and other recipients of welfare. At the same time, women united to fight for money for nurseries, for shelters for battered women, rape crisis and other resource centres for women; which women themselves could control. Only after 1974, with the adoption by the women's movement of the demand for legal and financial independence for women, did sections of the women's movement begin to fight for state policies which legislated for equality, ones which treated women (and children) as independent persons in relation to benefits, taxation and law. Fran Bennett discusses this strategy, and in particular the problems of legislating for women's independence in a situation of underlying inequality, where the established power relations of gender already privilege men in employment and at home. Such problems illustrate again the interconnections between work and home. To be effective, changes in state policy must tie up with changing women's conditions at 'work', a restructuring of working lives, and changing men's attitudes to child-care and housework. Struggles for individual rights are also but one aspect of a broader feminist vision which is both autonomous and communal. It seeks fundamental social change which could integrate work, family life and community, where flexible social provision would enable the affectionate and caring relations, *assumed* to exist in the family, to extend far beyond individual households.

Did the women's movement make a mistake in attacking conventional family patterns? It is true that while many more people now oppose the most blatant sexist practices – rape and violence against women – and support women's rights to contraception and abortion, women's situation generally has not changed much. In fact, together with all other oppressed groups, women's situation has deteriorated with the continuing economic recession. Since 1978, women's wages have been falling even further behind those of men. Women remain poorer than men and poorer than they were ten years ago. And women are the first affected by welfare cuts. In this climate, anti-feminism and conservative appeals to strengthen the family can gain ground. Women themselves may feel that 'liberation' is a con, worsening their situation. Our supposed equal rights have been used to let men off the hook in relation to contraception, wife and child maintenance. They seem to mean little in a situation of more fundamental inequality, where women's lives are still controlled by our domestic roles.

So women may look back to an imagined more secure past. But in fact the past was never secure, as women and children have never been adequately protected by male wages. (The tens of thousands of women forced into prostitution in Victorian London expose the myth of the good old days. Feminists were *not* wrong to attack conventional family patterns. Indeed, far from us now accepting the inevitability of traditional family arrangements, we can see that our struggle for equality has been undermined by the failure of the trade unions and the socialist movement to pursue changes in employment, social policy and welfare that would enable new types of domestic arrangement. Women's greater vulnerability today, as yesterday, is the price we pay for the fact that *our domestic role has not changed*. (Even though household structures and employment patterns have.)

So women remain disadvantaged in waged work and still shouldering vastly unequal burdens of domestic work. (Working or not, women do 80 per cent of domestic chores.[6] At work the concept of the 'family wage' has protected the interests of male workers at the expense of female, though only 5 per cent of male workers entirely support dependent wives and children.) We know that until men's attitudes to domestic work change – and trade unions make the links between work and home, demanding working conditions adjusted to domestic needs to enable men and women each to participate fully in both spheres – then male privilege at home and work remains unchallenged. Moreover, appeals to strengthen the family in the context of cuts, assume that women could take on additional caring services in the home, for the old, disabled and ill, when in fact many could not even if they wished. Without women's wages, four times as many families would live in poverty. Such appeals also strengthen the neglect of those who live outside traditional families. This includes single parents, gay people, the elderly, women whose incomes crucially support themselves and other dependants: in fact, *over 70 per cent of all households*.[7]

No amount of pressure to strengthen traditional ideas on women's place in the family can really succeed today. (Indeed, the decline of traditional family households has been the most significant trend in domestic life over the past fifteen years, as the number of people living alone and of single parents have doubled.[8]) Women will *not* retire from waged work. Many could not even if they wished to. Women *will* still seek to control their fertility and fight for sexual autonomy. They always have, whether using old potions for fertility, birth control and abortion, risking death through back-street abortion or fighting for safe, free, legal abortion. Some women *are* still choosing to have children outside of marriage, to live together and build new supportive networks and communities. Glorification of the traditional family will not abolish these choices. They reflect wider changes in capitalism itself. But what such glorification can ensure is that we make our 'choices' in conditions which impoverish our lives and those of our children, increasing the stress and strains on households. We know, anyway, that families with young children are more financially handicapped than those without, and they are often the ones where men work the longest hours of overtime. We know, too, that single parents, nearly one family in three in Inner London,[9] are the most financially deprived.

The point is that the 'ideal family' is no longer typical; it functions as myth. Family ideology needs to change, so that 'the family' no longer suggests the married heterosexual couple with children, dependent on a male wage, but instead a variety of possible family forms.

There are certain types of 'families' which certainly do need defending – single parents and their children, gay couples and lesbian mothers – but they are under attack *because* they do not conform to the family ideal. Black families, too, need defending. They need defending against racist immigration laws where the hypocrisy and cynicism of the British state in its commitment to 'the family' is most blatantly revealed, as it keeps apart wives from husbands, grandparents from kin, and is prepared to separate mother from child. The family the British state claims to care about is a white family.

But there is a terrible hypocrisy behind our present government's 'concern for the family', when we know that all types of household live in poverty and neglect, and prominent among these are those with young children. Attempts to solve this by looking back to a supposedly more satisfactory traditional family, where women were both dependent and subordinate, can solve none of our problems today. 'Family policies' and trade-union demands which recognize and support the *variety* of ways we now live and care for each other, where men and society generally assume responsibility with women for child-care, domestic life and the care of all dependent people, could move towards solving many of our 'family' problems. This would mean adequate incomes and services, shorter working hours and realistic child benefits, operating in the context of a caring society where men as well as women know the meaning of caring. Then those same family values of love, care and commitment which, if seen as the individual responsibility of women, are oppressive, could extend beyond the confines of gender and home to become an essential part of a society which would liberate us all.

Notes and References

1. Quoted in *Woman's Own*, 28 April 1979.
2. At the Conservative Central Council Annual Conference, Solihull, 24 March 1979, quoted from Bary King, 'The Image of the Family in Thatcherism' (unpublished paper).
3. A. Levitan and R. S. Belous, *What's Happening to the American Family?*, Johns Hopkins University Press, 1982.
4. M. Nava, 'The Family: A Critique of Certain Features', in M. Wandor (ed.), *The Body Politic*, Stage 1, 1972.
5. D. Dinnerstein, *The Mermaid and the Minotaur*, University of California Press, 1976; N. Chodorow, *Reproduction of Mothering*, University of California Press, 1978.
6. Source: Department of Employment, *Manpower Paper*, No. 11.
7. Figures cited from Lesley Rimmer, *Families in Focus*, Study Commission on the Family, London, 1981.
8. See *Happy Families?*, Study Commission on the Family, London, 1980, p. 17.
9. Rimmer, *Families in Focus*, p. 43.

2 'Smash the Family?' Recalling the 1960s

LYNNE SEGAL

When, pregnant and fearful, blackmailed by both my parents, I reluctantly married in 1968, I felt for certain that my action was unprincipled and wrong. I told none of my friends. I lay silently sulking for the rest of the day. It was not, however, any early waves of feminism that triggered my self-reproach – though I would like to think so. It was rather the critique of marriage and the family which I had absorbed from the circles I moved in throughout the 1960s.

My friend, pregnant at the same time, remained unmarried. More daring than me, delivering her son at home alone with a pair of scissors, she later suffered all sorts of indignities from many sources as an unmarried mother. Like me she believed that to marry (or even go to hospital) was to allow the state to control you. It was to enter the bourgeois world – not our world. Even to seek support from the father of your child was bourgeois! As a single parent in the early 1970s, however, financially secure and living collectively, I was able to raise my son in what I still firmly believe were ideal conditions for both of us, with the help of many friends – another product of the ideas some of us shared in the late 1960s.

Without any doubt, many of the radical ideas from that time were self-righteous and simplistic – a product of youth and privilege, confined mainly to an ex-student metropolitan milieu. But, something did happen in the 1960s. And I want to sketch out what it was, to look at the cultural and political climate of that time in order to see how it came to inspire such great hopes for change. What happened was something which affected the way in which a significant, vociferous and boisterous minority of mostly young people began to look at many, almost all, of the central institutions which shape our lives. The family, the school, the university, the factory, the community, prisons, mental hospitals: something was very wrong with them all. Something was wrong with the state, wrong with the world. '*Do not adjust your minds, there is a fault in reality*.' So the 1960s abounded with criticisms of 'the family', that social arrangement in which we are all supposed to live. Pessimistic anxiety about the nature of family life was certainly not new, firmly pushed aside though it had been for a time in the post-war years. What was dramatic about the criticisms which came out of the 1960s, though, was that, for a while, some of us used them to conclude that we must and could fundamentally *change* things. We could begin immediately to change our own lives, if not the world.

To see behind the ebullient optimism, as well as the chaos and disorder, which characterized the final years of the protest movement of the 1960s and early 1970s, we need to return to the birth of that generation which participated: a generation whose birth itself, as the 'bulge' generation, was a celebration of the thankful return to a 'new and better' family life for all. For the Second World War, like the first, had transformed people's family lives. Home life was no longer the husband and wife living together and raising their children, economically dependent primarily on the man's wage, and held together by the woman's work in the home – the central idea of the Western family form for the last hundred years. Husbands were far from home, and wives worked for long hours in a wide variety of jobs, with the help of state-funded nurseries, canteens and better health care. But those soldiers who did return in 1945, returned with high hopes for a better life, and above all eager to embrace 'the comforts of home', to secure their traditional roles. Men wanted the jobs women had filled, and married women were expected, and indeed sometimes eager, to return to the home, to resume as central their roles as wife and mother.[1] They, too, wanted something *new*, after the war had ended. War-time nurseries and canteens were closed, despite some resistance from women.[2] The family re-formed itself.

Reconstructing the Family

And the family was itself reformed – with renewed ideological support from every quarter, and a new material support from the state. Indeed, there developed a new and obsessive concern with the importance and sanctity of family life – a concern, however, which spotlighted almost exclusively the role of women in the family: women as mothers; women as domestic consumers. Though the state had been forced to increase its provision for women and children during the war, it was after the war that it became clearer that the support the state would offer the nuclear family was part and parcel of its attempts to strengthen women's role and duties in relation to children. Maternity benefit and child allowance both reflected the state's interest in women's central role as mothers, spurred on by racist and imperialist fears of a falling white British birth rate. Beveridge, in his Report of 1942, which became the blueprint for the post-war Welfare State, is explicit on these points. 'The attitude of the housewife to gainful employment outside the home is not and should not be the same as that of the single woman. She has other duties . . .'[3]

These welfare allowances did minimally lessen women's economic vulnerability. But they carefully did not, to any significant extent, lessen the economic dependence of women and children on the perhaps precarious protection of the male breadwinner. Indeed, the welfare reforms of the 1940s and early 1950s more tightly entrenched the wife, as mother, in her dependency on the male wage-earner, by assuming in all circumstances – from taxation and insurance to benefits and grants – that a married woman and her children would be provided for by the husband.[4]

Many other factors served to intensify the exaltation of family and domesticity throughout the 1950s. The housewife in her suburban castle, however lonely, was aware that life held no greater joy than that of marriage and motherhood, from her daily diet of popular magazines, pop music and novels. Barbara Cartland reigned supreme, Daddy was home, and by the 1950s an all-embracing conservative consensus held sway throughout almost every Western country from Europe and the United States to far-away Australia. The new consensus was constructed from carefully orchestrated paranoia and illusion: a fear of the dangers of communism abroad and an illusion of harmony at home. The old antagonisms of class and sex were seen as 'removed' by the protective embrace of the Welfare State, and by increasing home-ownership in the working class. The consensus rested upon that grain of 'self-evident' truth, which can reshape all contradictions to create successful ideology.

The truth maintaining the façade at home was the reality of high employment, and of massively increased domestic consumption. These two factors worked together to support the huge economic expansion of the 1950s throughout the Western world. There was a continuously higher standard of living for most people in the 1950s and 1960s – with vacuum cleaners in most homes in the 1950s, and television in most homes in the 1960s. The inequalities between classes, however, remained the same. Tories and Labour alike, through thirteen years of unbroken Tory rule, fostered a belief in continuing progress, and an end to all conflict, from Macmillan's 'Never had it so good' slogan of 1957, to Crosland's 'post-capitalist society'. As Hobsbawm wrote, 'If ever capitalism looked like it worked, it was these decades.'[5] Indeed, an obsessive concern with status and appearance emerged in all classes as each family strove to realize

Sir Anthony Eden's Tory vision of a house-owning democracy.

What lay behind the 'affluence' and higher level of domestic consumption – quite apart from the fundamental but hidden decline of the British economy compared to other Western economies – was long hours of overtime worked by men and, despite the real force of the ideology of domesticity, the ever-increasing participation of married women in paid work. Contradictory though it may appear, the eulogy of hearth and home went along with an expanding labour market increasingly employing married women, once their children were at school. They worked to enrich the domestic budget. Nothing, however, was more central to the ideology of consensus, to the idea that the aspirations of all classes and groups now converged, than the notion of the *happy, healthy family*. As Elizabeth Wilson carefully outlines, 'The family was simply assumed as central by everyone, feminists included.'[6] Women's special role in the home was to be given a new status and importance.

In the relatively new and rapidly expanding social sciences of the 1950s, sociology, psychology and anthropology – whether in the work of Talcott Parsons, Winnicott or Murdock – the family, in its modern nuclear form, was presented as universal and eternal. So, rejecting previous anthropological and historical evidence, George Murdock assured his readers in 1949: 'The nuclear family is a universal human social grouping.'[7] As well, we were assured, it served to provide a refuge and haven in the increasingly complex, stressful and meaningless world of work and the city, while allowing for the expression of 'natural' sexual differences – women's 'expressiveness' and men's 'instrumentality'. So convincing was the new family ideology, combined with statistics which showed a high level of marriages and a declining number of divorces (following the post-war divorce 'peak' of 1947), that in 1958 the Church of England Moral Welfare Council was able to conclude, 'the modern family is in some ways in a stronger position than it has been in any period in our history of which we have knowledge'.[8]

Meanwhile, a lot of very hard work was necessary to maintain the belief. In fact, Daddy's homecoming, to wives and children he barely knew, had led to high levels of marital rift and crisis, while many women were at least vaguely aware of the narrowness and isolation of their renewed domestic lives. Accordingly, the 1940s and 1950s also saw the growth of a new concern by the state to intervene to prevent the breakdown of marriages. The Denning Report of 1947 was the landmark establishing the principle that: 'The unity of the family is so important that, when parties are estranged, reconciliation should be attempted in every case where there is a prospect of success.' Moreover: 'It should be recognized as a function of the State to give every encouragement and, where appropriate, financial assistance to marriage guidance as a form of Social Service.'[9]

Home Office grants have been offered to various marriage counselling services ever since. More generally, the rapid expansion of professional social work had, as its main focus, the maintenance of traditional family life, which, as Jeffrey Weeks has stated, 'was curiously seen both as "natural" and permanent and as fragile and threatened'.[10] One new ingredient to postwar marriage counselling was a greater emphasis on mutual sexual enjoyment, with the acceptance of Kinsey's finding that female physiological sexual responsiveness was the same as that of the male.

The most powerful ideological support for traditional family structures in the 1940s and 1950s, however, was the widely popularized interpretations of Freudian, particularly Kleinian, views on the mother–child relationship. Ironically, as part of a new permissive emphasis on the child and on the importance of the mother's role, John Bowlby in Britain and Benjamin Spock in the United States also induced considerable anxiety in parents, but mostly in mothers, by emphasizing the psychological dangers of any kind of inadequate maternal care creating 'irreparable harm' in the child.[11] On these views, a mother's personal growth and happiness, as well as her child's, were seen as intrinsically linked to her relation to her child, rather than any wider relationships. 'Working mothers' faced both double workloads and moral guilt. Fathers were given little role in this domestic scenario, though women were to make sure that they did not feel threatened by the passionate mother–child bond. A labour of love, indeed!

Ironically, it was from here, in the revolt against the all-consuming, possessive and demanding mother, that one of the main critiques of the family in the 1960s was launched. But there were many other contradictions about to engulf the new image of the happy family. Though the children of the early 1950s had been described as the 'Quiet Generation', at least in the United States,[12] a new and noisy lot of near monsters was about to emerge from its cosy nest. For among the children of the 1950s, both working and middle class, many were to grow up in the 1960s to detest the narrow and confined lives of their parents, to despise their acquisitiveness and conformity, and to resent their protectiveness.

The Divided Family

In the 1960s, then, the dominant theme to trouble and titillate the minds of the virtuous was the 'generation gap'. Youth were in revolt against their parents, though it took a few years for Roger Daltrey to stutter out on their behalf (in The Who's 'My Generation'):

> Why don't you all f-f-fade away
> Don't try to dig what we all s-s-say

to his climax:

> Hope I die before I get old.

He didn't, though Keith Moon did, and Pete Townshend nearly did. And in retrospect, it is easy to piece together the inevitability of the various strands of youth protest to emerge in the 1960s.

There was little continuity from the youthful struggle of our parents to survive and raise their children through the hard work and sacrifice forced upon most people in the 1930s and 1940s, to the new values of consumer capitalism which developed with the relative prosperity of the 1950s. It was, in fact, capitalism itself which was to discover and build a new cult of youth aimed at the 'teenage consumer' with more money to spend, and more easily able to spend it. A necessary part of this process was the switch from an emphasis on hard work and saving towards pleasure, excitement and self-fulfilment in leisure activities – as radio and television brought the advertising industry and pop music into every home in the country.

It was the emergence of predominantly white, male, working-class subcultures – among youth whose 'relative deprivation' contrasted most with assumed affluence – that was to create the first of the post-war 'moral panics'. There was the threat of the Teddy Boys in the mid 1950s, jiving to Bill Haley and then to the more blatantly phallic sexuality of Elvis. The media feasted on the spectacle of teenage violence and sex. With the 1960s came the Rockers, proudly proletarian, asserting territorial divisions, chauvinistic and into rock music, motor-cycles, black leather and swastikas. They saw themselves as distinct from, and with the help of the media could be whipped up into conflict with, the Mods, seen as upwardly mobile, super-cool, hip youth into smart clothes, pep pills, soul music, ska and scooters covered with lamps.[13]

Common to both youth subcultures, however, was the feeling of difference from the parent culture, with a distinct style and fashion to prove it. These boys no longer spent their leisure time with dad in the local pub, but blasted out on sex, sound and drugs.

Other looser and overlapping subcultures, associated more with urban middle-class youth, were soon to emerge in Britain and elsewhere. 'Right, everybody clap your hands, And DO ANYTHING THAT YOU WANT TO DO', sang out the thirteen-year-old Stevie Wonder, topping charts round the world in 1960. And what the kids wanted to do was get high, get laid, groove to the beat, and reject every aspect of the straight world of their parents. They needed some money, supplied by parents or casual jobs, usually added to by state grants for higher education. They rejected ambition, acquisitiveness and work. It was sick to be ambitious, joining the suckers to work. Freedom meant expressing yourself and having fun; *SELF-EMANCIPATION*. John Lennon was 'trying to find out what is real in me and make it evident'; Mick Jagger, 'against anything that interferes with individual freedom'; Eric Burdon's religion said, 'Have a good time without harming anyone else.'[14] The Beatles, the Rolling Stones, the Animals, sold swinging, permissive London to the world in the mid 1960s. 'All you need is love.' So it seemed, in the carefree world of Western middle-class and many working-class youth – the great increase in the support for higher education meant that the student population quadrupled between the 1940s and 1960s, giving so many more young people the space between school and later jobs to enjoy themselves, whether as hippies, wierdos, freaks or simply swinging students. 'She's leaving home', as the Beatles put it, for the one thing that sacrifice and money can't buy. '*She's having fun.*'

The wave of hedonism and egalitarianism which swept over the country in the 1960s was real enough. It was no longer necessary for actors, as in the past, to get rid of their regional or working-class accents. On the contrary, Albert Finney and Michael Caine were to use them as passports to fame, so long as

'Charlie Bubbles' and 'Alfie' were at least trying to combine sex and fun with their good fortune. What was less clear was the link, if any, between youth protest, doing your own thing, trusting your own feelings, refusing to be thirty, and any wider class or political struggle, or any permanent rejection of marriage, the family and other institutions of bourgeois life. There was a link. But it took the whole decade to mature. Not surprisingly, in the meantime, moral panic rose over youthful 'sexual depravity', drug taking and hedonism. Increasing 'permissiveness', with the promotion of the contraceptive pill, the relaxing of censorship laws in 1961, abortion and homosexual law reform in 1967, and the liberalization of divorce in 1969, led many a Jeremiah to prophesy the collapse of marriage and family life.

Some sociologists of the early 1960s, like Ronald Fletcher, hastened to the defence of the nuclear family, suggesting an increased cooperation and affection between husband and wife.[15] Fletcher did admit, on the other hand, that the greater intimacy and privacy of today's nuclear family was 'potentially unstable', while 'stresses and strains' were caused both by women's greater economic independence and by mutual expectations of sexual and romantic love within marriage. As well, he argued, the smaller number of children in families could lead to an over-concentration on and high expectations of each child, producing anxieties in parents and child alike, while older people, increasingly separated from kin, experienced great loneliness.

Fletcher's qualified optimism was soon replaced by a steady flow of pessimism on the state of the family within the social sciences throughout the 1960s. In the United States, Keniston, Slater, Lidz, Bateson, Sennett and others wrote of the stifling inward-looking nature of the post-war family.[16] In their view, having left the big cities for the suburbs, the typical family unit was more isolated than ever, separated from kinfolk and community. The family group itself became the whole social world for its members, expected to provide the diversity and novelty of social relations in general. In fact, it encouraged passivity, apathy and indifference to the wider world. Material possessions provided its only stimulation. This is what the kids were rejecting, they said, as they migrated back into the cities in search of stimulation.

By the early 1970s, most popular American texts on the family, reflecting the debate of the 1960s, argued the need for change in family structures, whether through the abandonment of compulsive monogamy, a return to extended families, collective living, or changing the division of labour within households.[17] In Britain, Lomas, writing in 1967, reported 'widespread ill-health and unhappiness in families'. Again he described the 'unreceptive, rigid, defensive atmosphere' which 'stifles the child', as a result of the social isolation of the family group.[18] And in the oft-quoted Reith Lecture of 1967, Edmund Leach described the inward-looking family with its intense emotional stress generated between husband and wife, parents and children, in even more dire terms: 'Far from being the basis of the good society, the family, with its narrow privacy and tawdry secrets, is the source of all our discontents.'[19]

It is a bitter irony that, throughout the 1960s, politicians of all shades continued to promote the post-war break-up of old communities and industries to New Towns, while sociologists and psychiatrists were busy describing the isolation and dislocation such policies produced. Though Crosland could boast as late as 1971 that most people did not want more community participation but preferred to lead a 'full family life and cultivate their gardens', leaving power and politics to others, the kids had long since left the garden and the bloom had been seen to fade.[20] Most people did still continue to *seek* all their fulfilment in their family lives, but the 1960s had begun to expose the frustrations and pains of that search.

Without a doubt, though, in England it was R. D. Laing who

fired the imagination of the growing section of more educated
youth and became a guru of the protest movement. '*The dreadful
has already happened.*' And it happened in the mad world of the
family. At the beginning of the 1960s, Laing had provided a
moving account of the brutality of standard psychiatric practice
in its labelling and treatment of mental illness. He had argued
that the irrational behaviour of schizophrenics was intelligible
once looked at in the interpersonal context of the family, in
which it originated. It was intelligible once we entered the
phenomenological world of the patient whose strivings towards
autonomy were most often crushed by the overprotective,
smothering mother who could not leave her child alone. For
example, in his first book the schizophrenic patient Julie
believed that 'a child (probably herself) had been murdered'.[21]
In an existential sense this was true, said Laing. She had never
been able to become a person.

By 1964, Laing, with Esterson,[22] had decided that schizo-
phrenia was not any sort of identifiable condition or disease at
all, but rather the only possible way certain children had been
able to cope with the unrealistic, demanding, confused and
contradictory messages from their parents. Children in today's
small nuclear families have no one to turn to but their parents,
and are trained never to trust anyone outside of the family.
Once again, it was the unhappy, insecure, cold, but possessive
mother on whom Laing focused, as preventing any possible
autonomy or authenticity in her daughters' behaviour. Laing
did not, however, analyse the specific position or frustrations
of women in the family, which might shed light on their over-
possessive, troubled relationships with their children.

By 1965, Laing, in his most popular book, which became a
best-seller, along with Cooper and many of his friends and
followers, had come to the conclusion that: 'We are all murderers
and prostitutes', are all 'bemused and crazed creatures, strangers
to our true selves . . .' Adaptation is adaptation to 'a world

gone mad'.[23] The function of the family is to repress sexuality, for the sake of security, 'to create, in short, one-dimensional man: to promote respect, conformity, obedience'.[24] Perhaps, Laing suggested, 'madness' is the only sane response to an irrational world, a potentially healing process. Perhaps the 'schizophrenic' who rejects our stunted 'normality' is beginning to see the light. On Laing's account, not only are 'normal' people all impoverished products of capitalism, but they are all responsible for accepting our 'industrial-military complex', and the threat of thermonuclear war.

At the close of the decade, in *The Politics of the Family*, Laing attempted to outline the 'operations' through which the family destroys and mystifies its own children. Presided over by parents who are themselves insecure, anxious, bored and frightened, the family, as the only secure refuge, must be preserved *at all cost*. Unaware of the unstated rules which govern family life, children are ascribed characters from the parents' own set of family relationships (Johnny, who is artistic, is a little mad like his mother's father, the artist). Children are induced to conform to attributions provided by the projection or 'mapping' of family scripts over many generations. 'It's my impression that we receive most of our earliest and most lasting instructions in the form of attributions,' says Laing. The love which the parent bestows on the child is a form of violence, in that it is not freely given, but more like an invasion to create in the child the person the parent wishes to see: 'families, schools, churches are the slaughterhouses of our children.'[25] Increasingly damnatory, Laing's books became so popular simply because many young people could identify with them.

Lessons from Abroad

Yet Laing's writings were also moulded by the ever more extreme and apocalyptic rhetoric of the late 1960s. This was a rhetoric so all-embracing and total as to demand a complete 'revolution of every-day life'. It happened like this. After a decade of political silence, the close of the 1950s had seen the rebirth of protest with the rapid growth of CND (Campaign for Nuclear Disarmament) from 1958. Thousands of people, particularly young people, broke free from the 'dull and dreary fifties' to join the festive and joyful Aldermaston marches against the bomb. These marches were soon to provoke the first large-scale state violence of the 1960s, when hundreds were arrested defying a march ban on processions in late 1961. But the CND movement was to decline, disillusioned, after the Labour Party, having pledged support for unilateral disarmament, reversed its policy in 1961. Some veteran CND campaigners, like Jeff Nuttall, saw the self-indulgence of the young in the 1960s as 'a part of the sickness attendant on living with the bomb', and their aggressive cynicism as a product of the failure of the movement against it.[26]

Politically quiet once again, Britain saw from afar the momentous civil rights movement in the United States, where, for a while, black and white people fought together against the relentless racist discrimination in the South. In 1961, Bob Dylan arrived in Greenwich Village, soon to become an international prophet of protest as people memorized his songs, at that time of moral outrage over racial atrocities, nuclear catastrophe and war: 'Now is the time for your tears.'

Poverty as well as racism was rediscovered in the 1960s. Michael Harrington popularized the plight of the 'invisible' 40 million who lived in poverty in America, while Richard Titmuss and Peter Townsend exposed deprivation and need in Britain. In the United States in the early 1960s, many young people went to do community work and organizing among the poor, or joined Kennedy's Peace Corps, supposedly to assist poorer countries. Increasingly, however, the brutal reality of American imperialism in maintaining super-exploitation and oppression in the 'Third World' was brought home to young Americans. There were guerrilla struggles throughout Latin America in the early 1960s following the Cuban Revolution in 1959. Many Americans were shocked by the Cuban missile crisis in 1962 when Kennedy threatened nuclear war against Cuba. Students began to attack the Cold War ideology, blaming America not Russia for the arms race.

The American civil rights movement and its development into a black movement was to be of profound significance for the Left in both the United States and Britain. In 1963, Martin Luther King was addressing audiences of 250,000. Increasingly militant, the black movement was to abandon the old civil rights approach with the assassination of Malcom X and the outburst of black riots in Watts and Los Angeles in 1965, when over thirty black people were killed by police and national guardsmen. In 1966, Stokeley Carmichael and others formed the Black Panther Party, and by 1967 the black ghettoes were in revolt in Newark and Detroit, while black leaders were jailed and killed.

The most powerful of all the politicizing forces in the United States in the 1960s, however, were, of course, the Vietnam War and the draft. Both escalated in 1965. It was Vietnam which brought together the young drop-outs and hippies with political protest. As Abbie Hoffman wrote in 1968 as he was organizing, in his way, to get the acid-heads and flower children to march with the anti-war movement in Chicago: 'Look, you want to have more fun, you want to get laid more, you want to turn on with your friends, you want an outlet for your creativity, then get out of school, quit your job. Come and help build and defend the society you want.'[27] Do what you want AND fuck the system.

Hoffman's politics were the politics of ecstasy, the 'psychedelic revolution' of Timothy Leary to spread peace and happiness by expanding consciousness: 'Turn on, tune in, drop out.' But it was also Jerry Rubin's 'violent revolution'. 'Burning money, looting and shop-lifting can get you high.'[28] Politics became street action theatre. Hoffman and Rubin invented 'yippies', to use the media to spread revolution. America was soon revealed as the Land of the Pig. Everywhere people had been beaten up, arrested, and were soon to be shot (at Kent State University) for protesting against the war. (The war can only be defeated at home, said Nixon, and to some extent, it was.)

Abbie Hoffman had been a psychologist and in the American New Left of the 1960s. In some ways, like its smaller equivalent in Britain, the American New Left tried to create a socialist theory which rejected traditional Marxism, 'the dead weight of the past', for what was seen as more relevant to the present situation: questions of culture, consumption and control over one's life. A chief educator of the New Left was Herbert Marcuse. The central question for Marcuse was that of 'domination'. Contemporary capitalism operated with new forces of repression, creating 'false needs' for commodities whose satisfaction produced the passive, quiescent 'one-dimensional man', interested only in consumption and the symbols of affluence. The modern technology of capitalism controls through the manipulation of needs, and was repressive alike of man's real instinctual drives, and of nature. It was 'irrational as a whole'.[29]

So, for the New Left, political struggle was inseparable from personal liberation. It was about the loneliness, anxiety and futility of everyday life under capitalism, about developing new needs and acting in new ways. Politics was linked to sexuality, to finding a new sensuality that could eroticize all social relations, including those of work. It was about understanding the impossible sexual longings aroused and left unsatisfied by the false permissiveness of capitalism's manipulation of genital sexuality. The working class, Marcuse believed, had come to accept and defend capitalism. Revolution would come from those on the outside – black people, the unemployed, students. It would come through the 'Great Refusal' – a complete rejection of everything, including the mechanisms for political change allowed within this capitalist system. Marcuse was later to talk of the 'heroic period' of the hippies and yippies.

And heroic at least some of the dreams of the hippies had been. The Diggers of Haight Ashbury in California, for instance, had attempted to create a totally free cooperative community, providing free shelter, food and legal advice to all who needed them. Sections of the anti-war and hippie movement were united in their search for a new way of life, a new cooperative society. America was to become one big happy family, instead of the isolated, sexually frustrated, fragmented families at war with each other and the world. Along these lines, Rubin was to describe imperialism and Vietnam as a 'supermasculinity' trip, the product of 'sexual insecurity'; and the America of his dreams as 'one big commune with free food and housing, everything shared'.[30]

By the end of the 1960s, there were 10,000 communal households in the American census.[31] Most of these were urban communes where people, not related by blood or marriage, lived together supposedly cooperatively. Between 1965 and 1970, it is estimated that between 2,000 and 3,000 groups left the cities to set up rural communes in the United States. Many of these were fleeing from police harassment of urban communes. The aim of many of them was to be self-sufficient. They wanted to return to a simpler, more integrated and meaningful life, and, whatever their particular goals, all of them shared a desire to live and raise their children more collectively within a larger community to which they could feel *connected* and *belong*. The communal movement wanted meaningful work, creative schooling and an alternative to the repressive destructive 'monster' it believed America to have become.[32]

Students Erupt

By the spring of 1968, the student movement *internationally* was in revolt. The Berkley Free Speech Movement of 1964 was only the beginning of and an inspiration for the growth of direct action by students everywhere. Students were rejecting the 'education' imposed by authoritarian universities, demanding teaching which was both meaningful to them and committed. 'The tigers of wrath are wiser than the horses of instruction,' Blake had inspired them. They hoped to be 'the catalysts for change in the world'.

German students, like American students moved by anti-imperialist struggles abroad, formed the 'anti-authoritarian' movement. They wanted to connect up the violence of imperialism with an exposure of the 'invisible' violence and authoritarianism of their own society. It didn't take long. By 1967, a German student had been shot dead while demonstrating against the Shah of Iran. And yet it was students who were branded as 'terrorists' and 'parasites' by the German Springer Press monopoly. In April 1968, the student leader Rudi Dutschke was shot in the head by a young fascist. It was Dutschke who had first talked of the 'long march through the institutions' – the setting up of socialist or red bases of popular control within each institution. When he was shot, tens of thousands of students took to the streets. The German state responded by drawing up 'emergency laws' similar to those Hitler had used, which were to provoke massive occupations of universities in almost every city by May 1968.

Even more spectacular was the revolutionary struggle of May 1968 in France. Ten million workers were on strike, demanding higher wages, shorter hours and more union rights, and hundreds of colleges, factories and work-places everywhere were occupied. They had been provoked into action initially by escalating police brutality against anti-imperialist students, who were also demanding greater control of their universities. For two weeks, France seemed on the verge of revolution. Militant students and workers alike were demanding 'autogestion' or self-management. Then de Gaulle dissolved the National Assembly to call new elections which in late June gave him a landslide victory. The Left had been in disarray and divided, while the press united behind de Gaulle. The Communist Party, and therefore the main trade-union federation, were also determined to return things to normal by ordering workers, many of whom had won huge concessions and wage rises, back to their jobs. The spontaneity and direct democracy of the militant students and a section of the workers, inevitably volatile and hard to sustain, could in no way withstand the forces they were up against.

For many, though, May 1968 remained the peak of struggle for a new way of life and a new society. Daniel Cohn-Bendit, with his brother, was still to conclude, after the defeat of May, 'between us we can change this rotten society' if we can 'learn to love', to abolish leadership and hierarchy, and act 'with others, not for them . . . There is only one reason for being a revolutionary – because it is the best way to live.'[33] Cohn-Bendit was to return to his native Germany for collective living, shared child-care and community organizing.

According to the Ehrenreichs, while German and French students were in revolt, 'the English left looked on admiringly'.[34] In fact, during 1968 there *were* scattered but important student struggles in Britain. The Revolutionary Socialist Students Federation was formed that year to coordinate activity on the 'red bases' where student struggles were occurring. The aims of the federation were for students to win democratic control over higher education, to build student power in support of working-class and anti-imperialist struggles, and to fight racism in Britain. (The year 1968 was that of Powell's racist attack on immigrants, forecasting future race wars.)

As with students everywhere, the demands for collective democratic control over your own life and work, and for an end to conforming passivity, were fundamental. And the notion of 'sexual freedom' was intrinsic to the struggle. 'An alert student leadership can show the concealed systematic relationship between sexual controls, university authoritarianism, economic exploitation, and imperialist aggression.'[35] The family was seen as a repressive institution for transmitting the alienated and hierarchical relations of capitalism, and robbing sex of its eroticism.

Not just Marcuse and Laing, but also the ideas of Wilhelm Reich, Malcom X and the Situationists became popular among students in the late 1960s. Reich's *The Function of the Orgasm* became a best-seller when reissued in the 1960s. Reich's theory of the orgasm, first developed in the 1920s, was basic to all his work. In it he argued that *all* psychic disturbance resulted from some disturbance of orgastic potency, and its cure depended directly upon 'the possibility for establishing the capacity for full genital satisfaction'. Fiercely heterosexual and anti-gay, Reich saw satisfaction as not simply a product of orgasm, but the 'capacity for surrender to the flow of biological energy without any inhibition', free of fantasy and guilt.[36] Reich also spoke of specific character structure or character armour, physical blocks and tensions, produced by repressed sexuality. These served in a negative way to prevent people from experiencing life, both within and without, in its full intensity.

Reich saw *the authoritarian family* as responsible for instilling sexual inhibitions in the first place. Moreover, he said, the function of such repression is political. Thus, Reich had written in the 1930s, the family's 'cardinal function, that for which it is mostly supported and defended by conservative science and law, is that of serving as a factory for authoritarian ideologies and conservative structures . . .'[37] So Reich believed that the suppression of the child's natural sexuality was political, in that it created adults who were shy, obedient, passive, fearful of all critical and rebellious thoughts and committed to supporting authoritarian structures. Sexual liberation and the destruction of the authoritarian family were therefore essential to political struggle and human liberation.

The inspiration of Malcom X, Franz Fanon and other black writers lay in their emphasis on the psychological oppression of centuries of global white supremacy, as well as the economic exploitation of capitalism. This, in turn, created new forms of militant cultural as well as economic struggle. Black people had been left out of history, stripped of their culture, internalized feelings of inferiority and guilt. Malcom X had written of 'the deafness, dumbness and blindness that was affecting the black race in America'.[38] Black militants also stressed the necessity of violence, for black rage, to create effective revolutionaries. Fanon wrote of violence as a 'cleansing force'. 'It frees the native from his inferiority complex and from his despair and inaction.'[39]

Finally, the small but megalomaniac Situationist International, founded in Paris in 1957, was to provide the rhetorical profundity behind many a 1968 slogan. Inspired by Dada and surrealism, they attacked every aspect of contemporary capitalist life and culture. More contemptuous than Marcuse, they saw everyone 'hypnotized by work and by comfort', obsessed with 'garbage'. Life is reduced to a mere 'spectacle', controlled by bureaucrats, where work is meaningless. Like Marcuse again, or their own original mentor, Henri Lefebvre, they argued that the 'poverty of everyday life' could only be fought with a new spiritual attitude, 'by making our unconscious desires conscious, and by creating entirely new ones'.[40] 'Everyone must search for what they love, for what attracts them.'[41] Everyday life must be transformed, not through theoretical debate and abstraction, but through passionate, subversive acts. So, Raoul Vaneigem argued, life must become an 'endless banquet', with pleasure as its only guide. 'There are no limits to creativity. There is no end to subversion.' Hence the indefatigable graffiti artists, with their giant slogans, from Nanterre to Columbia. 'Never Work.' 'Boredom is counter-revolutionary.' 'Live in the Present.' 'Take your Desires for Reality.' 'Be Realistic, Demand the Impossible.'

The Counter-Culture

In Britain, as elsewhere, it was outrage over Vietnam, and Wilson's tacit support for American aggression, that most clearly united the hippie psychedelic culture of drugs and music with the more political protest movement. Both contributed to Britain's counter-culture which flourished between 1967 and 1971, combining alternative life-styles and politics.

In July 1967, the Vietnam Solidarity Campaign (VSC) held a march of a few hundred people. But by March 1968, 20,000 demonstrated outside the American Embassy, with Mick Jagger marching with them. By October of that year, 100,000 people joined the third massive march against US imperialism in Vietnam. 'THIS YEAR OF DISGRACE' the *Evening News* called it, inventing, with the rest of the press, 'scenes of riot and terrorism'. Meanwhile the underground press and other institutions of the counter-culture were emerging in Britain.

IT, begun in October 1966, was England's first underground or alternative paper, combining 'art politics sexuality pop'. After its second police bust in 1967, one of its editors, John McGrath, summed up the new movement *IT* represented. It was inner-directed, permissive and more a movement of celebration than of protest. It had no leaders, individuals trusted themselves. It was 'optimistic' while 'slowly, carelessly constructing an alternative society. It is international inter-racial, equisexual with ease.'[42]

Release was also formed in 1966, to give advice and legal aid to drug-users, and more ambitiously, *BIT*, as a twenty-four-hour information and coordinating service, encouraging the alternative society 'to act as a society with responsibility for each other'. The following year *OZ* began its English career as an alternative porno, satirical, subversive magazine; and Cooper, Laing and others organized the 'Dialectics of Liberation' conference at the Roundhouse to analyse 'destruction' – psychic, racial, ecological and imperialist, seeing them all as connected. The first arts lab was opened in 1967 in Drury Lane, and by 1969 there were 150 such alternative culture centres.

Free pop concerts, 'legalize pot' campaigns and psychedelic shops, on the one hand, urban and rural communes, squatting campaigns and claimants' unions on the other, all became part of the newly emerging alternative culture – *a new way of living*. The counter-culture was to be the refuge *against* families, against work, against straight careers, bourgeois status and achievement – and increasingly, against police repression. The underground, wrote Richard Neville, did not work 'except for fun'. People lived in communes, outside 'the outmoded family structure'. Children in communes in most respects 'belong to all'.[43]

As in the United States and Europe, the commune movement was an integral part of the counter-culture in Britain. Since the traditional nuclear family was seen as a central bulwark of hierarchical, class society, it was essential to establish the possibility of alternatives. 'I would see the continued existence of the bourgeois family unit – which Reich called the compulsive marriage – as the largest single block to a radically new state of affairs in this country and throughout the Western world,' the editor of the underground paper *INK* declared.[44] It is hard to estimate the number of people who actually were living collectively, sharing housing and ideally housework and chores. All the underground papers, *IT*, *OZ*, *Frendz*, had readers seeking membership of them. Those who have studied the commune movement in Britain report how commune members saw themselves as providing examples for others, proving that there was a better, more caring, more cooperative way to live. 'I personally feel that while it is absolutely necessary to engage oneself in class struggle, it is also necessary to develop in one's own life the human values of socialism,' wrote Laura Ross from the Newhaven Commune.[45]

Commune life was building the new society in the shell of the old: 'You are changing society every day as you live your life ... living and acting the way I do I influence people ...'[46] 'The alternative society means caring about one another and sharing.'[47] Many of the more permanent urban communes were involved in local politics, working on alternative papers, in left presses or other self-help projects. In these communes, members usually ate together of an evening, contributed to a household kitty, held regular meetings for collective decisions and relied upon rotas for cooking, babysitting, shopping and cleaning. They saw themselves as leading richer lives, which at the same time allowed more energy for other things, while strengthening a radical oppositional culture and life-style. Both men and particularly women emphasized the importance of communes in providing collective child-care and a healthier and livelier world for children and mothers.[48]

More ambitious than the urban communes were the rural collectives and the official Commune Movement. There were at least fifty rural collectives, many attempting to be self-sufficient through craftwork and farming. They were proudly utopian, seeking a federation of communes, interconnected by need and mutual aid. Yet many communes, particularly urban ones, were fairly short-lived. The main problems were, first, economic, and secondly lack of privacy, jealousy, personality clashes and conflicts over sharing.

A more dramatic example of the underground life-style/political struggle was the London Street Commune which squatted 144 Piccadilly in late 1969, arousing press hysteria, and swift, violent action from the police. The aim of the Street Commune was to 'return the streets to the people', to provide a real escape route for the kids outside of the family, the schools, and all other repressive institutions which tried to 'tame and contain' them.[49] That same year, squatting groups, especially in Ilford and Notting Hill, began moving homeless families into empty property, protesting about the 100,000 homeless people and 500,000 empty houses in London.

By the end of the 1960s, the continual merging of self-absorbed hedonism and political protest with the passionate rejection of every aspect of bourgeois society became ever more ardent and explosive. People faced mounting police repression and raids, as black people, youth, women and the unemployed began to organize themselves. These were the groups most affected by the beginnings of the economic recession, and ignored by the Labour Movement. Military struggle re-emerged in Northern Ireland as the Catholic community, protesting against savage discrimination and oppression, was met with assassination and bullets. A more macho, warlike, paranoid and desperate politics came to the fore.

The Angry Brigade was about to begin its bombing campaign, to spread their illusion that 'The AB is the man or woman sitting next to you. They have guns in their pockets and anger in their minds' (Communiqué 9). Men wanted 'shooters' as well as orgasms. The two became enmeshed in the notion of 'armed love', to strengthen 'the people' and terrify the bourgeoisie. Illegality became not so much an act to fight and expose the class basis of bourgeois law, as a necessary thrill. 'Crime is the highest form of sensuality.' Passivity and boredom, seen as the twin evils destroying us, were to be fought with the combined weapons of the gangster and the lunatic. 'Madness has become in our age a kind of lost truth.' Spirals of cynicism, despair, addiction and real madness did overtake a few of the 1960s rebels. Others turned to mysticism. Some found new collective identity and meaning in the emerging industrial struggles and the growth of the shop stewards movement, joined Left groups, or the autonomous liberation movements of the early 1970s, particularly as gays, women or unemployed.

The Silence of Women

Women. Where were women during the 1960s? It really is astonishing how little we produced during the radical movements of that time. No woman spoke at the 'Dialectics of Liberation' conference. Women did not speak for the hippies, yippies or Situationists. Though Angela Davis spoke for black people; in the United States, white women were even denied a platform in anti-draft meetings despite the enormous work they put into draft resistance.[50] With the few exceptions of Betty Friedan's pioneering work on the misery of the American housewife, and, less well known, a few articles here,[51] women remained politically silent till near the close of the decade.

It was not just that it was men who said and wrote almost everything. Nor just that the goal of 'sexual revolution' basic to the counter-culture was to intensify women's position as little more than sex objects for men. It was also that 'mother', that 'manipulative, incestuously demanding mother',[52] – mother who can only smother – was the target of so much ambivalent aggression. For she was the home, the family, the straight world, from which the young boys just had to escape, 'Billy Liar', 'Morgan', 'Alfie', 'Lucky Jim' and all. The girls had to escape too, if we were to enjoy the new sexual freedom, such as it was. But sexual protest, assertiveness and the search for orgasmic sex is not so new for young men, whereas it was certainly harder for women to feel confident in their role within it.

Most popular culture of the 1960s was also silent on or told us little of women's lives and struggles. The best-sellers of the decade portrayed men's battles with insane authorities, with convention, with the dreary constraints of work, marriage and family life. Joseph Heller's *Catch-22*, perhaps the single most popular book of the early 1960s, describes Yossarian's paranoia as he battles helplessly with military officialdom. Corrupt and ridiculous, the army is not only a threat to one's life, but can even interfere with a man's favourite pastime – whoring. At the same time, Kesey's hero, in *One Flew over the Cuckoo's Nest*, takes on the sexless, bullying, fanatical 'bitch' who runs his psychiatric ward, while exposing the barbarism and brutality of the mental asylum.

Portnoy, in Philip Roth's best-seller *Portnoy's Complaint* at the close of the 1960s, battles through his shrink with his Oedipally possessive Jewish mother. While Mailer, the chest-thumping megalomaniac archetypal male of the 1960s, tells us in his many books just where a man should whop his cock, or occasionally a knife, if he was to stand up to the American totalitarian nightmare and insist again that 'violence was linked with creativity, and adventure was the secret of love'. Mailer, like Dylan, Donleavy, Cleaver and Sinclair (of the American White Panthers), equated rebellion with renewed assertion of conventional masculine arrogance and aggression, complete with its contempt for women and homosexuals. Women as wives, women as mothers, who require commitments and make demands on a man, are part of the problem. Or sometimes they could be romanticized as Earth Mothers, 'sad-eyed ladies' or sexy chicks, so long as they could appreciate the struggles of the man – sorting through the bitches who don't for the bitches who do.

In films as well 'it was a man's decade in the movies'.[53] Man as anti-hero, outlaw, madman or simply loser, won the hearts of his audience. 'When he's robbed a few banks he'll feel better,' says Paul Newman in *Butch Cassidy and the Sundance Kid*. Their female companion, Katherine Ross, neither heroine nor anti-heroine but there to praise and protect the heroes' masculinity, articulates the 1960s contempt for the always pitiable woman-without-a-man; 'I'm twenty-six, and I'm single, and I'm a school-teacher. And that's the pits.' Adding, as she agrees to flee the law with the two male buddies, roughly, 'So I'll go with you. And I'll cook, and I'll clean. I'll wash your socks, and I won't moan. Only one thing I won't do. I won't watch you die.' Cooking and cleaning for a man, whatever the circumstances, is obviously preferable to being a spinster teacher. So much for the trendy androgyny, the supposed withering away of all social roles, including sex roles, in 1960s rebellion. And here, too, the dread of female ageing. For a woman to have reached her mid-twenties was to be sinking fast.

Indeed, the veneration of youth, and dread of ageing, particularly in women, was an important theme of the 1960s – like Tom Wolfe's story of Donna, a twenty-one-year-old surfie girl said to have killed herself, her life having come to an end because she was twenty-one. No longer could she be one of Wolfe's 'flaming little buds'. Female fashion and sexual allure in the 1960s became increasingly pubescent. Mary Quant ('pornography is great . . . only ugliness is obscene') told us in 1969 that the bust is out in fashion because 'the bosom is a motherhood symbol'. Mothers were out, raw Twiggies were in. Indeed, older women, as shown in the use of Bette Davis and Joan Crawford in such films as *Baby Jane*, were clearly obscene. The teenage Lolita, semi-virginal but eager for sex, was the ideal sex object of the sexually permissive 1960s. Her extreme youth and lack of experience meant her assumed eagerness for sex did not threaten the man's sexual superiority. The expression of sexual desires in older women, however, presented just such a threat, and was therefore rendered comic or neurotic, as in *MASH* or *The Graduate*.

Expressing agonizingly well the male attitudes women accepted in the 1960s, Edna O'Brien explained to Nell Dunn that women expected too much. They should learn to do without. We could not blame men for women's sorrows when, for example, it is both inevitable and natural that men should abandon older women to pursue young women. When an older man fancies a young woman, 'you know that he has every right to . . .', because women age sooner. Indeed, 'it's this fleetingness of girlhood that's one of the saddest things in life. It's sad for girls, it's sad for men. It's the peak of a girl's life, her budding, whereas it's not the peak of a man's life.' [54] Such was the anguish of the 'sexually liberated' and perceptive woman of the 1960s, inevitably seeing through the eyes of men.

The main contradiction for the 'liberated' woman of the 1960s was undoubtedly the equation of 'sexual liberation' with freedom. Thus Margaret Drabble wrote in 1969, 'Emancipation is now a reality', and woman 'is free now, as never before';[55] she meant, free to fuck and not get pregnant. For liberals and radicals alike, sexual pleasure was the source of the drive towards liberation, towards transforming all human relations. 'MAKING LOVE IS GOOD IN ITSELF AND THE MORE IT HAPPENS IN ANY WAY POSSIBLE OR CONCEIVABLE BE-TWEEN AS MANY PEOPLE AS POSSIBLE MORE AND MORE OF THE TIME, SO MUCH THE BETTER.' [56] To the radicals, marriage and the family systematically destroyed this subversive potential of sex. Couples were also seen by some as oppressive, creating possessiveness, jealousy and exclusiveness.

To understand women's situation in the counter-culture, is to understand its strengths and its weaknesses. Defining women's liberation in sexual terms, with the aid of more efficient contraception, did liberate women from certain sexual constraints, but not from sexual subordination to men. The problem was obscured by our common-sense, biological or in-stinctive conception of sexuality, as something which is either expressed, in full orgiastic release, or else repressed. This drive-reduction model of sexual behaviour was characteristic of the Freudian and even more strongly the Reichian conception of libido. Physiological approaches also characterized the very in-fluential American sexologists, Kinsey, Masters and John-son. Yet, there is no evidence for some *physical* sexual need, comparable to hunger or thirst, which if not satisfied has patho-logical consequences. Even more mystifying, sexual behaviour, seen as the physical release of energy, is not seen in terms of social relations. Seeing sexual behaviour in terms of instinctual liberation, or physical gratification, merely reinforces rather than examines the existing patterns of domination now accom-panying a heterosexuality where the penis is seen as an instru-ment of conquest and women as sex objects.

Thus Richard Neville in *Play Power* (Penis Power?) can illus-trate the private revolution in sexual attitudes by his own 'hurricane fuck' of a 'cherubic 14-year-old' school-girl. 'No feigned love or hollow promises.'[57] Ideal sex here resembles male masturbation and fear of women, more than anything likely to give emotional, or even physical, pleasure to women. Men's attitudes to sex at this time hardly suggested new and less alienated forms of sexual relationships. This is hardly sur-prising, when sexual behaviour was seen as 'natural', rather than as expressing the power relations between men and women. Wide-eyed and innocent of such things, Neville describes 'gang-bangs' with gusto, and likens the media's taste for violence to 'an old lady yelling "rape! – please" '.[58] 'Infants,' he believes, 'get the most out of their sex life.'[59] Or, as Nuttall's friend assured him, 'One can have a good fuck without even touching the other person.'[60] Quite! But men's stunted and sexist erotic life, excused in the name of liberation, was one problem – only to surface with the growth of the women's movement. The related desire to avoid any deep emotional commitments, also in the name of liberation, was as central to the problem of women in the counter-culture.

It related to a deep-rooted dilemma in all radical movements over the last two centuries: that of individualism *versus* collectivism. Young people were indeed searching for a new type of *community* as they left the suburbs, many for more collective living situations in the city. They not only often sought to build more caring relations with others, but learnt to resist and fight for change – particularly through an identification with the most oppressed, the most victimized in capitalist society. This identification with the *lumpen*, with those, like students themselves, outside of and largely ignored by the traditional structures of the Labour Movement, was what lay behind many of the *collective* struggles around squatting, the formation of claimants' unions, prisoner support groups, youth work and support for anti-imperialist struggles. There was an imaginative and creative side to many of these struggles, largely because they occurred outside the traditional Labour Movement: a Labour Movement, together with its political organ, the Labour Party, at this time rightly seen as solidly entrenched in its support of national and international capitalism.

But more negatively, the stress on self-expression, spontaneity and total rejection of everything bourgeois could also lead to a conservative *individualism*. Stressing the importance of the individual could be progressive in its emphasis on self-discovery and the need to affirm the political significance of our conscious choices, and our individual desires and imagination. But it could also be conservative in its assumption of some ultimate individual experience of self which was seen, as was sexual desire, as existing somehow outside history and culture.

Being radical: being myself. Anything which separates me from myself oppresses . . . Not only bourgeois morality oppresses, but any morality which imposes oughts from outside . . . Not only the middle-class role playing is oppressive, but attempting any kind of role, even the role of radical intellectual.[61]

But what is this 'radical' self which transcends or lies outside of bourgeois morality, of all social determination? Whatever it is, most people, we were told, had 'lost touch' with it. Therefore revolutionaries must not only attack the structures of capitalism, but also liberate people by blowing their minds, shattering and disrupting everyday expectations. The picture is of a sort of vanguard of liberated spirits, slowly, by their exemplary rebellious behaviour, liberating the rest. Laing and his many followers shared this mystical conception of the liberated self and how to reach it. 'If I could turn you on, if I could drive you out of your wretched mind, if I could tell you I would let you know.' What? What would they let us know? According to Cooper, and Laing would agree, they would make us see the importance of 'experiencing one's aloneness in the world', of accepting one's separateness, no matter how lonely the trip; 'in the end all you have is yourself'. We must separate out that part of ourself that has been constructed ('invaded') by others, and return to the self that is ours alone[62] – the atomized individual of capitalism in search of freedom!

The ideal was to be emotionally *independent*. In the spirit of the 1960s, 'true love' does not expect reciprocation. That women, in their roles as girl-friends, wives and mothers have always been doing most of the emotional giving and nurturing, which men have been receiving while characteristically providing less adequate nurturing in return, was something which was simply mystified in the accepted wisdom of men's emotional independence and women's greater dependence. *Women*, as Edna O'Brien illustrated, needed to change. No doubt children also needed to change their dependency needs. Indeed, cats were a great favourite at this time, seen as so emotionally 'independent'.

But the idea of us all existing as independent atoms, rather than existing essentially in relation to others, caring and inter-dependent, is obviously at the heart of the bourgeois values of capitalism. These values were important. They were important in holding out the promise of a personal freedom to control our lives – a promise which in reality capitalism itself frustrates. People do not control their working lives, the economy, nor even understand the nature of the capitalist state. These values are also limited. They are limited in their focus on individuals and their rights and interests, rather than on any overall vision of a free and equal society. The individualistic vision of people ultimately alone in the world and responsible only for themselves, struggling for self-knowledge and self-fulfilment, is clearly not the collective vision of socialism. This is a vision where self-expression accepts responsibility for others and unites with others against social forces which restrict human potential and happiness.

It is not even in any sense true that we *could* exist as independent atoms. Every aspect of our experience of ourselves and others is determined by our contacts with others. Without the experience of secure, caring relations with others, we could have no stable identities at all. Indeed, Russell Jacoby argues that to prescribe total subjectivity as a basis for social liberation is to prescribe the illness of capitalism, our sense of psychic isolation, as its cure.[63]

The idea of self-emancipation, which fitted men's own illu-sion of themselves as 'independent' and unattached, fed women's sense of inadequacy. And women did feel subordinate to men in the 1960s. They were mostly marginal to the struggles and felt it. As Bea Campbell recalls, 'I wasn't a student, or a man, or black; so the very energy of the explosion of '68 just seemed to complete my sense of political marginality and lone-liness.'[64] Sex was a problem – most women recalling the 1960s speak of an active sex-life, where they were personally passive. Sex just happened. Anya Meulenbelt described how she lived through her male lovers throughout the 1960s and would,

> Breathe and drink theatre if he is a theatre person. Live politics if he is in politics. Am interested in art if he is a sculptor. I don't understand how other women can do without, how they can live alone, or with a colourless husband.[65]

So the 1960s' stress on the politics of self-exploration was contradictory. It did feed into a movement for change. Treating all social relations as political, including how we relate to and care for each other, did enable more people to connect up their own lives, frustration and sense of personal failure with the need to change society. It also produced a new understanding of *oppression*. It revealed the complexity of economic, cultural, political and legal domination behind existing power relations, as well as the self-hatred and fear accompanying subordination. By the end of the 1960s, women and gay people in particular were analysing their oppression as a group, as had black people before them.

The stress on direct action from below and the general attack on all forms of authoritarianism did encourage the growth of personal autonomy and resistance. It led to an analysis of both direct and indirect forms of state coercion, from the police and army through to welfare, schools and clinics; as well as to a rejection of the dogma and hierarchy of Left groups, the rigidity of trade-union structures and the reliance on experts in every field. As Sheila Rowbotham wrote of this time: 'I realized that my actions were important. We were all capable and responsible for our politics. I think such a feeling was peculiar to 1968.'[66]

Where it all led, as we have seen, was to the optimism and energy that went into creating 'alternatives' in every sphere, into 'struggling to change things now' – through self-organization and self-help. It was all both naïve and wrong in so far as it was believed, and it was, that these alternative structures could somehow expand to encompass and change the whole of society. But to the extent that these alternatives were able to suggest ways we could live and organize now more readily to meet our needs, they were important. Collective households, for example, did mean that young single people had more choice. Single women, in particular, at least in London, could choose to leave home, remain single, have an 'active sex-life', and also companionship. They need not live alone. Single mothers, even though typically taking on the primary mothering and housekeeping role, did often have some help with the baby-sitting, or, at the very least, more companionship in raising their children. But the value attached to self-fulfilment and autonomy meant that collective households mostly remained loose and impermanent. At any time, individuals would feel free to leave, creating insecurity and tension.

There were definite limits to accepted permissiveness in the 1960s. Though marriage was no longer necessary for sex, there was still a very real stigma attached to unmarried mothers. Yet men could more easily opt out of paternal responsibility, both financial and emotional ('She should have used the pill'), leaving many women with children more precarious and vulnerable than ever. In the political communes, mothers were usually more fortunate, but, because of their needs for support and security, still remained the most vulnerable and easily exploited of its members. Collective living clearly could not solve women's general economic, social, sexual and psychological inequality in the world at large, and many communes, not surprisingly, reflected established sexual divisions of labour. Thus Abrams and McCulloch report that the commonest worry of women in communes was of their men leaving them.[67] A lot of the politics of the 1960s were linked to being young. What happens when you realize you won't die before you get old? The possible impermanence of collective households created anxieties, particularly as people grew older.

So alternative households, even if sharing housework and child-care, did not always manage to eliminate the male dominance of conventional families, nor to abolish all anxieties about the future, to abolish conflict and provide permanence and security. Though marriage today also has not abolished conflict and insecurity, we at least know it is *supposed* to. This has led some former radicals to reject the possibility of creating alternatives to conventional family patterns. It might, of course, only point to the difficulties of creating such structures, without more fundamental social change, especially at a time when sexism and the particular needs of women and children were only just beginning to be reassessed. As one 1960s' rebel, still living collectively today, suggests:

When you are walking, running, crawling away from what you know you can't go back to, which is the social structure handed to us by our parents' generation, what we move towards is something so unknown, so unsupported by the social structure we live in, with the whole capitalist structure working against it, that every time you get something together it is not surprising it can easily collapse.[68]

Undoubtedly the pressures on the nuclear family, so starkly described in the 1960s, remain with us today. The loneliness and depression of women confined at home, men's absence from home and women's over-dependence on children who come to resent it, together with the lack of any larger community for intimacy and companionship, all continue to undermine family life. The *need* for alternatives is as strong as ever, even though it is true that the space for experiment, and dreams of success, have shrunk as the economic recession saps resources and energy. Yet those of us who are still striving to change family life know that we need as much as ever today the support of forms of self-help and networks of friends, as well as to feel a part of an oppositional culture – ideals so much a part of the wisdom of the sixties.

And certainly, it was the growth of political struggle around personal life which had set the stage for the growth of the women's movement. The sense of inferiority and confusion which women felt in the 1960s, ever more blatantly consumed yet degraded as sex objects, praised yet abandoned as strong and autonomous rebels, pushed women ineluctably towards finding each other and finding a voice. Yet those same 1960s' ideals which rejected marriage and bourgeois values in search of a wider collectivity were also to inspire the early waves of feminism. Feminism was to be the fastest-growing movement of the 1970s – building on the creative strengths of the 1960s and embracing many of its problems, especially concerning notions of liberated sexuality and relationships. It also began anew the task of analysing women's situation in the family.

Notes and References

1. See E. Wilson, *Only Halfway to Paradise*, Tavistock Publications, London, 1980.
2. See D. Riley, 'War in the Nursery', in *Feminist Review*, No. 2, 1979.
3. As quoted in E. Wilson, *Women and the Welfare State*, Tavistock Publications, London, 1977, p. 152.
4. See J. Brophy and C. Smart, 'The Position of Women and Family Law', in *Feminist Review*, No. 9, 1981.
5. E. Hobsbawm, '1968 – A Retrospective', in *Marxism Today*, May 1978.
6. Wilson, *Only Halfway to Paradise*, p. 168.
7. As quoted in A. Oakley, *Subject Women*, Martin Robertson, Oxford, 1981, p. 238.
8. As quoted in G. Heath, *The Illusory Freedom*, Heinemann, London, 1978, p. 83.
9. From *Marriage Matters*, HMSO, London, 1979.
10. J. Weeks, *Sex, Politics and Society: The Regulation of Sexuality since 1800*, Longman, London, 1981, p. 235.
11. J. Bowlby, *Child Care and the Growth of Love*, Penguin Books, Harmondsworth, 1965.

12. K. Keniston, *The Uncommitted: Alienated Youth in American Society*, Dell, New York, 1960.

13. See S. Hall and T. Jefferson (eds.), *Resistance through Rituals*, Hutchinson, London, 1976.

14. Quotes from the Guardian Inquiry, *The Permissive Society*, Panther Books, London, 1969.

15. R. Fletcher, *The Family and Marriage*, Penguin Books, Harmondsworth, 1962.

16. Keniston, *The Uncommitted*; P. Slater, *The Pursuit of Loneliness*, Allen Lane, Harmondsworth, 1971; R. Sennett, *Families against the City*, Harvard University Press, 1970.

17. For example, A. Skolnick and J. H. Skolnick (eds.), *Family in Transition*, Little, Brown, Boston, Mass., 1977; H. A. Otto (ed.), *The Family in Search of a Future*, Appleton-Century-Crofts, New York, 1970.

18. P. Lomas (ed.), *The Predicament of the Family*, Hogarth Press, London, 1967.

19. As quoted in C. Gorman, *People Together*, Paladin, St Albans, 1975, p. 29.

20. A. Crosland, *A Social Democratic Britain*, Fabian Tract No. 404, Fabian Society, London, 1971.

21. R. D. Laing, *The Divided Self*, Tavistock Publications, London, 1960.

22. R. D. Laing and A. Esterson, *Sanity, Madness and the Family*, Tavistock Publications, London, 1964.

23. R. D. Laing, *The Politics of Experience*, Penguin Books, Harmondsworth, 1970, p. 2.

24. ibid., p. 55.

25. R. D. Laing, *The Politics of the Family*, Penguin Books, Harmondsworth, 1976, p. 91.

26. J. Nuttall, *Bomb Culture*, Paladin, St Albans, 1970.

27. A. Hoffman, *Revolution for the Hell of It*, Pocket Books, New York, 1970.

28. J. Rubin, *Do It!*, Jonathan Cape, London, 1970, p. 117.

29. H. Marcuse, *One Dimensional Man*, Sphere Books, London, 1964.

30. Rubin, *Do It!*, p. 256.

31. H. Seal, *Alternative Life Styles*, Prism Press, Dorchester, 1974.

32. See R. Houriet, *Getting Back Together*, Sphere Books, London, 1973.

33. D. and G. Cohn-Bendit, *Obsolete Communism. The Left-wing Alternative*, André Deutsch, London, 1968, p. 255.

34. B. J. Ehrenreich, *Long March, Short Spring*, Modern Reader, 1969, p. 103.

35. F. Halliday, 'Students of the World Unite', in A. Cockburn and R. Blackburn, *Student Power*, Penguin Books, Harmondsworth, 1969, p. 319.

36. W. Reich, *The Function of the Orgasm*, Panther Books, London, 1968, p. 114.

37. W. Reich, *The Sexual Revolution*, Noonday Press, New York, 1962, p. 72.
38. H. Malcolm and A. Haley, *The Autobiography of Malcolm X*, Penguin Books, Harmondsworth, 1968, p. 274.
39. F. Fanon, *The Wretched of the Earth*, MacGibbon & Kee, London, 1963, p. 74.
40. Quoted in C. Gray, *The Incomplete Work of the Situationists International*, Free Fall Press, Bristol, 1974, p. 2.
41. ibid., p. 151.
42. P. Stansill and D. Z. Mairowitz, *BAMN*, Penguin Books, Harmondsworth, 1971, p. 80.
43. R. Neville, *Play Power*, Vintage Books, London, 1971, p. 265.
44. J. Lloyd, 'Alternatives: Communes', in *INK*, 23 September 1971, p. 12.
45. Quoted in A. Rigby, *Alternative Realities*, Routledge & Kegan Paul, London, 1974, p. 19.
46. ibid., p. 36.
47. ibid., p. 64.
48. Based on personal experience and what sparse literature there is.
49. Stansill and Mairowitz, *BAMN*, p. 226.
50. See L. Cagan, 'Something New Emerges', in D. Cluster (ed.), *They Should Have Served that Cup of Coffee*, South End Press, Boston, Mass., 1979.
51. For example, J. Mitchell, 'Women: The Longest Revolution', in *New Left Review*, 1966; S. Gail, 'The Housewife', in Fraser (ed.), *Work*, Penguin Books, Harmondsworth, 1968.
52. D. Cooper, 'Saint Genet', *New Left Review*, No. 25, 1966.
53. M. Haskell, *From Reverence to Rape*, New English Library, London, 1974, p. 330.
54. In N. Dunn, *Talking to Women*, MacGibbon & Kee, London, 1965, p. 101.
55. M. Drabble in the Guardian Inquiry, *The Permissive Society*, pp. 26 and 27.
56. D. Cooper, *The Death of the Family*, Penguin Books, Harmondsworth, 1971, pp. 47 and 48.
57. Neville, *Play Power*, p. 74.
58. ibid., p. 21.
59. ibid., p. 274.
60. Nuttall, *Bomb Culture*, p. 219.
61. R. Aronson, 'Dear Herbert', in *Radical America*, vol. IV, No. 3, 1970, p. 13.
62. See Cooper, *The Death of the Family*, p. 11.
63. R. Jacoby, *Social Amnesia*, Beacon Press, Boston, Mass., 1975, p. 104.
64. B. Campbell, '1968 Retrospective', in *Red Rag*, 1978.
65. A. Meulenbelt, *The Shame is Over*, Women's Press, London, 1980, p. 86.

66. S. Robowtham, in *Red Rag*, 1978, p. 27.
67. P. Abrams and A. McCulloch, 'Men, Women and Communes', in Barker and Allen (eds.), *Sexual Divisions and Society*, Tavistock Publications, London, 1976.
68. From 'Living Your Politics. A Discussion on Collective Living: Ten Years On', in *Revolutionary Socialism*, No. 4, 1979.

3 From Utopian to Scientific Feminism? Early Feminist Critiques of the Family

MICA NAVA

With the development of the new wave of feminism in the late 1960s and early 1970s, 'the family' became a central focus of concern. It was perceived as the key institution in the determination and perpetuation of women's subordinate status. Thus, politically and theoretically, the new feminism distinguished itself from earlier feminisms which, it was felt, had tended to concentrate exclusively on women's rights and opportunities in the public sphere. The new feminism also developed its politics and theory in reaction and relation to the New Left, with which it had, and continued to have (particularly in Britain), a close association. In neither of these traditions had the family appeared as a critical arena.

So the initial attempts to understand women's oppression through an examination of the family were voyages of intellectual exploration and discovery. What made them uniquely dangerous and exciting was that they were rooted in and had implications for the way in which everyday lives were being lived. Thus not only did they emerge from the struggles to make sense of the complexities and frustrations of personal experience, many were also polemical and prescriptive in that they insisted on challenging the nature of existing familial relations.

What is interesting is that from these marginal, experiential and oppositional beginnings, feminist ideas about domestic life were, over the course of a few years, to become established as a new 'discourse' – a consolidated body of knowledge, institutionalized in feminist writing – which exercised power to define, regulate and disrupt modes of thinking and behaving. The process of this transformation is not easily theorized, and I shall do no more than draw attention to it.

What I shall do in this chapter is to document some of the key ideas which appear in the early critiques of the family and attempt to place them in a political and theoretical context. I shall indicate the way in which some of the early concerns were developed in subsequent and more elaborated feminist work. Certain themes were neglected in the early writing and received only perfunctory treatment in the intervening years; I shall draw out and analyse some of these gaps. I shall also discuss the utopian in feminist thought and the way in which this has shifted over the last fifteen years from the sphere of 'the family' to that of 'sexuality'. The morality inevitably embodied in some of the visionary writings and politics emerges as a kind of moralism, in that covertly it sets standards of personal conduct. I shall look at the contradictory impact that this phenomenon has had.

My choice of texts to illustrate these trends is bound to be selective, and my representation of them will be to some extent determined by my participation in this history. Thus I shall refer not only to what was written, but also on occasion to my memories of how the material was received. Overall, the emphasis will be on uncovering those aspects which can illuminate our understanding of the present rather than on attempting a total reconstruction of what was written and happened between 1969 and 1972 – the years on which I shall primarily focus.

1. 'The Personal is Political'

It is by now a commonplace to point out that feminism centre-staged the personal in a way which was unprecedented in political movements. It argued, first of all, that personal experiences were not individual isolated phenomena but the product of social circumstances which affect women in a systematic fashion. This was to be exposed in consciousness-raising groups through the examination of what had hitherto been considered too trivial to discuss in political terms: the minutiae of daily life. The other component of this centring on the personal was that private life became a legitimate object for 'public' scrutiny and evaluation.

It is from these two strands that the majority of the early critiques of the family were composed. In style they varied considerably. Many were founded on the experience of motherhood. Some were statements of despair or revelation. Others were more analytical, and I shall discuss the theoretical propositions in these later on. Here I want to concentrate on aspects of the political content and impact of the work (though, of course, it is impossible to draw a definitive line between the political and the theoretical). There is no doubt that in addition to trying to explicate personal experience, these articles had in common a major polemical objective: their overwhelming intent was not to engage in academic debates or to fill in the gaps in existing disciplines (which I shall argue became a dominant characteristic of subsequent analyses), it was rather to raise political consciousness so that people would act to change their lives. Thus a large proportion of these articles explicitly challenged the existing form and ideology of the 'nuclear family' – that is to say, the close and closed domestic unit composed of adult heterosexual monogamous couple and dependent children in which women were isolated from each other and responsible for child-care and housework – and frequently ended with proposals for alternative household organization.

The Utopian Vision

This imagined alternative household amounted to a utopian vision. In general, it proposed a unit much larger than the nuclear family; the pooling of labour, resources and responsibility; the abolition of power and economic dependency; the erosion of 'possessiveness' in personal relations both between lovers and between parents and children; and most importantly, the abolition of gender differentiation. This was not to be merely an alternative mode or a way of dropping out – part of the 1960s' counter-culture. A reorganization of this kind, it was often argued, would have multiple ramifications; it would in the end undermine the very foundations of capitalism. Many of the ideas were not new. Notions of pooling resources and eroding the economic power of the patriarch were present in nineteenth-century utopian and socialist schemes as well as in the ideals which informed the early development of the kibbutzim in Palestine in the first part of this century. Critiques of 'possessiveness' in personal relations were products of debates which culminated in the 1960s, though they started much earlier. In relation to children, the dominant influence was the anti-family perspective of Laing and Cooper.[1] Their proposition that children actually suffered from (became products of) excessively protective and insistent parenting was transformed from a negative critique of mothers, and appropriated by the early feminists in order to justify women's interest in loosening maternal bonds. Critiques of possessiveness in sexual relations were rooted in the counter-culture of the 1960s and neo-Reichianism, but were again transformed in order to illuminate the double sexual standards which operated both inside and outside marriage. Reich's theories about the politically conservative effects of sexual repression in children were made gender specific as part of a broader explanation for the more accommodating behaviour of women. Most important as well as specific to this new utopian vision was the insistence on the abolition of gender differentiation, particularly in housework and child-care. Men were to engage in the domestic sphere on equal terms with women.

It was this aspect which was quite unique in the history of socialist thought on the family. The dominance of ideologies about 'the natural' seems to have prevented the abolition of the sexual division of labour within the home from ever having been imagined. As a concept, it was absent from most early feminist writing. Sheila Rowbotham, for example (not a mother at the time), in her otherwise inspiring article 'Women's Liberation and the New Politics' (first published in 1969),[2] was remarkably moderate and traditionally socialist in her proposals for the family. She argued for more nurseries, launderettes and municipal restaurants rather than the entry of men into the domestic sphere. Margaret Benston (whose analysis of domestic labour I shall refer to later) in 1969 also argued for the socialization of child-care, cooking and so forth rather than increasing men's share of household responsibilities.[3] For many women in the early women's liberation movement, the issue was marginal to their lives. Yet for others, particularly those of us with young children, the issue of domestic responsibility was of overwhelming significance; the family was not only of theoretical interest, it was the sphere in which oppression was most excruciatingly experienced. Mothering was the linchpin.

Anna Coote and Beatrix Campbell have, in their recent book, identified two key events which they claim were responsible for the mobilization of women and their recruitment to feminism in the early days; these were the women's equal-pay strike at Ford's in 1968 and the Koedt article on 'The Myth of the Vaginal Orgasm' in 1969.[4] I suspect that one could produce dozens of women for whom the moment of illumination was prompted by another instance. For me, and probably many other mothers, the key influence was a relatively uncelebrated article, 'Child-rearing and Women's Liberation', written by Rochelle Wortis in 1969 and presented as a paper at the first Women's Liberation Conference in Oxford in 1970.[5] It was probably the first feminist critique of Bowlby's theories of maternal deprivation. In a measured academic style, Wortis pointed out that in some societies 'multiple attachments are the norm', and that what a child requires is a stable, sensitive, stimulating environment which can be provided by two or more people, male as well as female. Her conclusion was programmatic and polemical:

If the undervaluation of women in society is to end, we must begin at the beginning, by a more equitable distribution of labour around the child-rearing function and the home ... Men can and should take a more active part than they have done until now ...

The creation of alternative patterns of child-rearing ... is as much a political problem as an educational or psychosocial one ...

We cannot wait for the revolution before we change our lives, for surely changing our lives now is part of the revolutionary process.[6]

In today's climate, in which these ideas have become quite routine, it is hard to conceive the powerful impact this kind of analysis had. Notions about the dangers of maternal separation were so pervasive at the time that they had become part of common sense and were simply not questioned. The idea that men *must* take an equal part in child-care, and that this was not only *not* a trivial demand but part of the revolutionary process, seemed daring and exhilarating. It seemed a blindingly simple solution to the apparently irreconcilable needs of mothers, for time, and young children, for the kind of loving and consistent care rarely available in nurseries. (At the time, nursery provision was in any case only available to approximately 10 per cent of three- to five-year-olds, and practically non-existent for children younger than this.)

Yet, as I have already pointed out, an equal division of labour and responsibility between men and women within the domestic sphere was not always given priority or even considered in the emerging women's liberation movement. Indeed, even among those women for whom the experience of mothering and domesticity was totally enveloping, there was no consistent acceptance of the revolutionary nature of the rearrangement of domestic life. For many, it continued to appear as an individual solution, in spite of the rhetoric of the personal as political. The assertion that family change was political implied a substantive reassessment of what, for socialists, counted as politics. And this was only just beginning to happen.

These contradictions were manifested in another paper given at the Oxford Conference, written by Jan Williams, Hazel Twort and Ann Bachelli.[7] Each being mothers of two children, they presented an angry account of the 'martyrdom' and isolation of marriage, motherhood and housework and insisted that neither improvements in domestic technology nor women's entry into the labour market could offer a solution. Neither, interestingly, could men's equal participation in child-care: 'Man as mother as well as man as house-slave is no answer' because this would 'extend oppression'. The answer lay in communal living. Yet this also had limitations in that ultimately it remained an 'individual solution'.

Living in a commune must not be envisaged as a resolution to the housewife problem ... However women live ... their militant work must be governed by the imperative need to rouse the consciousness of their silent submerged sisters.[8]

The emphasis on communal living was equalled, then, by their emphasis on the importance of consciousness and personal change. The problem was stated incisively: 'The oppression that every woman suffers is deeply in her, she first has to realize this and then to fight it.'

Consciousness and Change

Williams *et al.* thus share with many other writers of the period the conviction that once ideologies of motherhood and child-care, so deeply internalized by women, were exposed as concepts which served only to subordinate them, the process of restructuring family life could be embarked upon. Not without a struggle, of course. But there is no doubt that it was felt that change depended largely on the *voluntarism* of women. We could do it if we wanted to. It had not happened before because we had been numbed by our conditioning. Because our newfound 'consciousness' had revealed to us the nature of our oppression as women in such a rapid and powerful fashion, it was assumed that the task was merely one of extending these insights to other women.

Yet, of course, these insights were not always unambiguously received, even among those women already committed to the women's liberation movement, *precisely* because they demanded not only a self-critique, silent or spoken, of a substantial portion of previous identities, but also because they implied a visible reorganization of domestic practices. Thus, for example, debates about the 'glorification of motherhood' were not unproblematically illuminating. The dilemma was not only to recognize our own complicity in tolerating what was suddenly so patently intolerable, but also how to distinguish between what of our old lives had to be jettisoned and what was worth keeping. How, for instance, were we to reconcile our rational critiques of a concept like maternal instinct with what seemed to many of us an indissoluble knot of passion for our children? And as I have already said, these early feminist critiques implied a change of practice as well as consciousness. This meant not only changing, but being seen to change. Although explicitly critical statements were not often made, it was clear that we both internalized the new criteria and used them as a basis for evaluating each other's living arrangements and relationships.

The following is an example of how this used to happen. Between about 1970 and 1972, women from the Belsize Lane Women's Liberation Group (of whom I was one) and our households were among a number of people who gathered on Hampstead Heath each fine Sunday to picnic and play volley-ball together. These gatherings were significant because the truth about the division of child-care within our living units was made quite public. Both men and women were, in a sense, on trial. If young children ran on to the volley-ball pitch and disrupted the game by crying for comfort from their mothers rather than their fathers or 'other friendly adults', we could feel quite exposed. This sort of occurrence seemed an almost shameful demonstration of our inability to progress beyond the stage of consciousness raising.

The political concern with consciousness and change found its theoretical expression within the early critiques of the family in their regular emphasis on 'conditioning' and 'socialization' as the key process in the construction of our acquiescence. The problem was to explain why we had failed to imagine that things could be otherwise. As Sheila Rowbotham put it:

Women have been lying low for so long most of us cannot imagine how to get up. We have apparently acquiesced always in the imperial game and are so perfectly colonized that we are unable to consult ourselves. Because the assumption does not occur to us, it does not occur to anyone else either.[9]

And Williams, Twort and Bachelli: 'Most of all it has been a sheer impossibility to imagine ourselves being involved in change of any sort.'[10]

Biological explanations were rejected early on. Freud's theories were unacceptable mainly for the concept of penis envy and the manner in which his psychoanalytic principles had been adapted in post-war US therapy, which, at its crudest, aimed to adjust a woman to the circumstances of her life. A third reason, though never as explicitly stated, was Freud's emphasis on the importance of the early development of children, which generated in its wake ideologies of appropriate maternal care. These rejections left us with a relatively non-contradictory and undynamic account of the development of femininity: sex-stereotyping arose from a process which included expectations, rewards, and identification with parental roles within the family; it was compounded by toys, schools and the media in 'society'. At the time, this model seemed sufficient. First of all, it explained cross-cultural variations (an area much researched in those days in order to substantiate our arguments against those who posited 'the naturalness' of gender difference and domestic organization).[11] Secondly, it seemed to be confirmed by our experience of personal transformation. As a profoundly 'social' explanation, it provided the opportunity for social intervention. It seemed, at this point, that ultimately the construction of gender difference was subject to our control.

In isolating men's entry into the domestic sphere, communal living, and consciousness, as the three key political features in the early texts, I have not exhausted the personal and programmatic elements in them—that is to say, those aspects which appealed directly to our sense of possibility and change. Some of the more 'analytical' features of the articles, such as, for example, reference to the nuclear family as a unit of consumption (to which I shall return later) were also subject to political resolution within the commune.[12] The texts were not *mainly* polemical and prescriptive. Yet, because they were so often rooted in our own domestic and emotional experiences (in a way in which analyses of women's class position, say, were not), they must be read in relation to the changes that were attempted as well as to the relative failures of these attempts.

Trials and Limitations

Before addressing the problems encountered in the practical implementation of the utopian vision, I want to examine more closely some of the proposals which were made. A general schema of the alternative household has been presented. Here I shall look at Shulamith Firestone's.[13] I have singled her out because her ' "dangerously Utopian" concrete proposals', as she herself called them, are the most detailed. In part of a lengthy section she argues for household contracts:

A group of ten or so consenting adults of varying ages could apply for a licence as a group in much the same way as a young couple today applies for a marriage licence, perhaps even undergoing some form of ritual ceremony, and then might proceed in the same way to set up house. The household licence would however only apply for a given period, perhaps seven to ten years, or whatever was decided on as the minimal time in which children needed a stable structure in which to grow up . . .[14]

Children would no longer be 'minors' under the patronage of 'parents' – they would have full rights . . . [For example] the right of immediate transfer: if the child for any reason did not like the household into which he [*sic*] had been born so arbitrarily, he would be helped to transfer out. An adult . . . [who might wish to do so] might have to present his case to the court, which would then decide as do divorce courts today . . . A certain number of transfers within the seven year period might be necessary for the smooth functioning of the household . . . however the unit . . . might have to place a ceiling on the number of transfers in or out, to avoid depletion, excessive growth, and/or friction.[15]

Considering how difficult it is for two people to commit themselves to each other and to sustain a relationship, the likelihood of ten people, 'of varying ages', simultaneously deciding that each others' nine best friends are also theirs, and that they are prepared to in effect 'marry' them for about ten years, is far-fetched to say the least. Implicit in Firestone's argument is the strange idea that all the individuals in this household will make decisions to undertake responsibility for children at the same

moment, so that at the end of the contract all the children will
be seven to ten years old, and old enough to make decisions
about where to live next (to form their own contracts perhaps?). It is also assumed that the abolition of the category
of minor will enable a child to reject its 'parents'. At the age
of two or three? How are the 'ceilings' to the number of
transfers to be determined and enforced? What happens if
everybody wants to leave and nobody is prepared to continue
to take responsibility for, say, four babies? The problems, of
course, are legion.

Firestone's programme was both more visionary and a great
deal less grounded in the *experience* of child-care and families
than were the British equivalents. (Hers was perhaps set further
in the future?)[16] All the same, this brief excerpt illuminates
some of the problems that had to be confronted by those who
attempted to implement the new ideals. It is quite impossible to
describe all the difficulties and contradictions here. Among the
most acute and time-consuming were probably those which
arose from the lack of rules and criteria available to help negotiate the new contexts in which traditional relations, expectations and modes of behaviour had been called into question.
Thus, in one celebrated commune in north London, an unwillingness to claim rights over property (rooms) or people (lovers)
meant that everyone regularly fell asleep around the kitchen
table. Living with several people was no guarantee of more
intimacy. On the contrary, it often led to an increase in personal
reserve. Nor was the promise of reducing domestic commitment
borne out: demands and confrontations were often multiplied.
Then there were the problems of unreconstituted consciousness: little girls still wanted to be princesses; principles about
reducing mother–child bonds and sharing out the cleaning were
sabotaged by uncooperative men; biological mothers occasionally reasserted proprietorial rights over their children and took
them from fellow-members of the collective household with

whom they had formed close ties. Traditional emotions like guilt, jealousy, dependence and resistance died hard.[17]

I certainly do not want to give the impression that all the experiences were negative and unproductive. In some cases satisfying solutions were worked out. What I want to stress are the tremendous difficulties encountered in attempting to live out the ideals. It was thus that the limitations of voluntarism became increasingly apparent. Gradually the utopian visions, with their implicit moral imperatives, were referred to with more scepticism; the optimism started to fade. Yet it still seemed impossible to develop a theory and critique of the family without conceptualizing alternative forms. An article which I think exemplifies the dilemmas of this transition period was written by me at the end of 1971.[18] Here I want to draw attention to its conclusion in which, in the style of the period, I offered the utopian proposals. 'How do I visualize the new ideal?' I speculated. What I, in fact, set out was more detailed than Wortis or Williams *et al.*, and far more constrained by what seemed *possible* than Firestone. What the proposals took into account were precisely the trials and failures of the previous few years. It was an attempt to reconcile the ideal with what our limits seemed to be. Group living, I suggested, was 'one *possible* alternative' to the limitations of the nuclear family; housework and child-care should be shared 'as equally as *possible*' (emphases added in 1982). Although a few moral imperatives remain – 'Marriage should be abolished' and 'children should not be economically dependent on their parents but on the group . . . all money and property should belong to the group' – these are tempered by an acknowledgement of the persistent nature of traditional personal relationships.

There is no doubt that in principle I passionately supported the idea of collective households. They seemed the only way of avoiding the negative aspects of the family while simultaneously retaining domestic life as a source of warmth and security.

Although particularly vital for women with young children, this way of living appeared capable of providing a solution to everybody's dilemmas. Yet, in spite of believing this, I concluded the article with a sceptical interrogation of the voluntaristic assumptions which had become so widespread:

What chance is there for any real change? On a personal level the way we live lags far behind our theories, old responses and resistances persist . . . Are we capable of acting upon and changing not only our ideas and our environment, but also our feelings?[19]

The problem remained 'in our heads', but was far more complexly and deeply embedded than we had anticipated. But it was still *women's consciousness* that was given priority as an object of political analysis and strategy. In my article there was no specific reference to the reluctance of fathers/husbands (as well as others, both men *and* women) to act upon their support for the principle of collective child-care, nor to the exercise of power by men.

Contradictory Repercussions

The particular emphasis in the early family critiques on change in consciousness and on programmes for prefigurative lifestyles (although crucial to the momentum of the movement and to the recruitment of women to it, in that consciousness-raising groups undoubtedly provided immediate rewards not available in more orthodox political organizations) thus also contained certain conceptual and political weaknesses. As I have already indicated, the complexity of psychic life, the resistance of men and the hazards of collective living were underestimated.

In addition, I would want to argue that ultimately the emphasis on personal change created limits to the political effectivity of the critiques. As prescriptions, they were pertinent mainly to (some) women in the movement. To the vast majority of women outside, they remained largely irrelevant. This is not to say that the analyses did not advance the debates both inside and outside feminism. They did. Outside the movement, it was to the Left in particular that the arguments were directed.

This historical association in Britain between the women's movement and the revolutionary Left – the determination to force the Left to take the politics of women's liberation seriously – was, I think it can be argued, another constraint. It was one of the factors responsible for the relative failure of the feminist family programmes to formulate proposals for welfare, legal and fiscal reform – to make demands of the state. Within revolutionary politics of the late 1960s, policy proposals of this kind were condemned as reformist and liberal, and were neglected.

However, this is certainly not to suggest that feminist political activity was confined only to 'changing the way we live'. Women in the movement were particularly active in a number of areas which emerged directly from the family critiques. Examples of these were the organization of collective child-care, crèches at conferences (the first in which men looked after the children was at the 1970 Oxford Conference), and community nurseries (for which demands were sometimes made of the local council). The first refuge for battered women was set up in 1971 (within five years, there were over fifty throughout Britain). This type of political activity was defined as grass-roots organization and thus escaped the label of 'reformist'. (Consciousness-raising groups had a more ambivalent response from the Left. They were sometimes virulently attacked by both men and women: feminists were described as 'objectively agents of the reactionary ruling class' who inhibited the revolutionary activity of the working class.)

Another consequence of the alignment of the women's movement to the revolutionary Left was its rejection of the capitalist press. This meant that feminist ideas were never really popularized. Accounts of women's liberation on the women's pages of the national press were invariably distorted, since we refused to write them ourselves, and then used as evidence of the implacable opposition of capitalism to the movement. In pointing to what I consider were some disadvantages arising from the early connections with the Left, I certainly do not want to exonerate the press which undoubtedly many times deliberately misconstrued what we had to say; I am arguing that to get them to report it right was not a priority. Nor do I want to suggest that anti-reformism was a strategy developed only out of the revolutionary politics of the previous decade. Over and over again in the women's movement, it was justified by reference to what was then conceived of as the failure of the suffragist 'single-issue' campaign, the failure to continue the struggle once the vote had been won (though subsequent research proved this assumption to be incorrect). Thus, in the early days, it was feared by some women that to fight for and win abortion on demand, for example, might be to defuse the broader political momentum of the movement. In this respect, Britain in the late 1960s and early 1970s was different from the United States. It had no equivalent to the active yet fairly traditional liberal feminist organizations, like the National Organization of Women (NOW), which although disregarded by socialist and radical feminists, were all the same successful in achieving reforms of significance for the lives of women outside the movement. In sum, the point I want to make here is that the *political* orientation of these early critiques, their demands for personal change rather than reform, can be argued to have limited their success in reaching beyond the confines of the movement in spite of the extraordinary intensity of the effect on those women within it.

I would like to draw attention to another unanticipated and adverse consequence of the particular personal and political emphases in these early family critiques. For several centuries family life has been subjected to moral evaluation (by the Left as well as by the Right). The complex interaction between this traditional moral resonance, criticized by feminists but ultimately only inverted rather than totally abandoned, and the feminist concentration on the personal, resulted in an unprecedented political phenomenon: the legitimation of judgements on the *person* and her *life*, in addition to her ideas and the political effectivity of her actions. This politicization of the personal was probably the major moral contribution of feminism. Its impact was enormous and led to an expansion of what counted as politics in both conceptual and practical terms. It was undoubtedly a progressive phenomenon; yet its effects were at the same time very contradictory. Both the confessional mode of consciousness-raising and the elevation of domestic life into an object available for scrutiny and assessment (in which good conduct could be awarded the metaphorical badge of the 'good feminist') were also profoundly *moralistic* and ultimately inhibiting. They emerged as a transmuted form of regulation.

Thus an inevitable aspect of the underbelly of the utopian programme, with its embedded assumptions of voluntarism and its particular analysis of consciousness (which took little account of the unconscious), is revealed as a moralistic censure of those who failed to achieve or attempt the vision. I am not suggesting that this censure was explicitly voiced in most instances. It was much more likely to take the form of self-criticism and guilt. Sisterhood in those days was more supportive than today; in the face of extensive external opposition, differences within the movement were minimized where possible. Paradoxically, it was perhaps precisely this mutual support (which, of course, in some ways contradicted yet also coexisted with the principle of public scrutiny), and therefore the lack of persistent investigation, which allowed these 'failures to live up to the ideal' to be attributed to individual inadequacies rather than collective theoretical and political errors (that is to say, the limitations of voluntarism and the difficulties of group living). In this instance, personal troubles were not transformed into public issues, they were not properly theorized. It was then supremely ironic, but perhaps to be predicted, that our attempts to overthrow the existing moral basis of family life succeeded only in shifting its axis. And as I have already suggested, the persistence of the moral ultimately inhibited further development of this strand of the family critiques. The visionary terrain was gradually evacuated.

I would want to argue that this occurrence marked a kind of crisis in feminist discourse on the family. It both provoked and demanded new ways of thinking about the problem. Thus, in the work that followed this period, the prescriptive was largely absent. Although moral and political considerations continued to act as underpinnings, they ceased to have the visibility that they had previously had. Subsequent writing tended to be analytical rather than polemical. Of course, the failure of the vision to resolve the dilemmas of the domestic lives of feminists was not the only factor to contribute to this change of style and direction. The year 1972 has been pinpointed as the one which saw the decline of post-1968 euphoria, the counter-culture and the first stage of the women's liberation movement.[20] With it came an increasing recognition of the need to extend the field of study, to develop both a more rigorous general theory and specific histories of operations and relations within the family and between the family and other social spheres. The shift from the visionary terrain and from a concern with the minutiae of daily experience was also a positive response to the tougher political context of the 1970s. In addition, there was an expansion of academic feminism in which the personal and the programmatic had no place. These factors combined during the 1970s with a more general social acceptance of marital dissolution and variations in domestic organization (to which, of course, feminist ideas had contributed).[21] One could speculate that the decline of feminist moralism in relation to the family was part of a wider transformation in which aspects of family life were decreasingly objects of moral evaluation.

The moratorium on prescription returned the organization of domestic life to the sphere of private unaccountable decision-making, though not necessarily to its nuclear form. It remains, of course, an essential feature of personal life to be negotiated by all feminists, and is undoubtedly negotiated with a changing battery of insights, principles and demands. But no longer is a single arrangement of living or child-care specified as the most apposite or correct in the struggle to advance the position of women.

Voluntarism and Sexuality

To conclude this section I want to draw attention to a more recent development within feminism which seems to echo many of the dilemmas I have already discussed. The decline in moral imperatives and assumptions of voluntarism in relation to domestic organization was followed a few years later by an upsurge of similar imperatives and assumptions in certain feminist accounts of sexuality (predominantly those of some radical and revolutionary feminists). In common with most other recent work on the subject, these accounts reject the 1960s biological-drive model in which sexuality was constantly pitting itself against societal constraints (though inconsistently, they often appear to hang on to these in their comments on male sexuality). They also reject psychoanalytical explanations[22] which emphasize the part played by the unconscious in the construction of sexual desire. In the manner of the early critiques of the family (though with a different object), these more recent feminist critiques have stressed the oppressive nature of both traditional and 'permissive' heterosexual relations, and have prescribed politically correct alternatives. For the critics of the nuclear family, the commune provided the utopian solution; similarly, for the critics of traditional sexual relations, the solution has become political lesbianism – that is to say, a distancing from 'male' modes of sexual expression and from relationships with men in order to advance the feminist struggle. Underpinning this ideal is the assumption that sexual desire is subject to rational political choice, echoing the voluntarism present in the family prescriptions.

Again, in the same way that private child-care arrangements were exposed to political scrutiny and judgement, women's sexual preferences have now become an indicator of the 'good feminist' – a legitimate object of political evaluation. In contrast, however, because positions within feminism are so much more polarized than fifteen years ago, there is no longer an impetus to minimize the censure for the sake of unity and sisterhood. In this recent expression of feminist utopianism, judgement is not always confined to 'incorrect' expressions of sexuality; it can be extended to include the whole woman. All aspects of her political contribution to the movement become available for criticism. This is not only a kind of sexual reductionism, it has become a new form of regulation.

Thus, as with the family critiques, I would want to argue that the effects of the voluntarism embodied in the political lesbian prescriptions must ultimately be inhibiting. Beatrix Campbell has suggested in an extended discussion of the subject that 'they deny any [feminist] political practice within heterosexuality and don't safeguard specifically lesbian culture and sex. They *prohibit* the formulation of a feminist sexual politics.'[23] At this point I have no explanation to offer for the displacement of the moral from the domestic sphere to the sexual. Whether or not the limitations of voluntarism and the contradictions of sexual life will become apparent – whether or not this approach to sexuality will undergo a decline to parallel that of the early family prescriptions – remains to be seen.

2. The Theoretical Contributions

A unique feature of the early women's liberation movement was its insistence on the fusion of the theoretical, the political and the personal. For the purpose of this chapter, I have attempted to unravel these strands, though no easy division can be made between them, and here my intention is to focus on the family critiques primarily as a body of theory. This will include looking at general assumptions and influences, and distinguishing between those areas of concern which subsequently were developed into major debates, and those which were dropped.

One of the significant characteristics of most of the early writing was its theoretical eclecticism. A number of different approaches were drawn on in order to tackle prevailing ideas which stressed the universality and inevitability of existing roles within the family, and the harmonious 'fit' between the nuclear family unit and modern industrial society. However, the overriding feminist concern was not to pinpoint the deficiencies of existing theoretical perspectives. It was to create a coherent explanation of all aspects of women's oppression, one which took into account the way the family operated economically and ideologically and the way in which it was experienced. For this project, theoretical purism was not a priority; and as well as focusing on diverse areas, the work combined a range of theoretical approaches (though differences between socialist and radical feminists were as yet uncrystallized). It also varied in its sophistication.[24] All the same, there were certain consistent patterns which emerged and continued to have political and theoretical consequences.

One of these was the notion of the family as a unit, a unity[25] encompassing different but complementary functions. This view was taken on by feminists from existing analyses and was then inverted. Thus, instead of being wholly good, the family became wholly bad. The tendency was to consider all aspects of it oppressive for women. Implicit in this kind of approach is the notion that progress can only be achieved if the family is totally destroyed. Minor reforms which benefit women tend to be undermined. Also undermined, I think, as a consequence of this totalistic view, are the positive features of parenting and intimacy which can occur in family life.

More important and more influential theoretically and politically was the feminist concentration on ideology as a *source* of women's oppression. In the late 1960s and early 1970s, this was in contrast to most Marxists, for whom the economic was the prime determinant of other aspects of society. But as Juliet Mitchell pointed out: 'There is nothing less "real" or "true" or important about the ideological than there is about the economic. Both determine our lives.'[26] And although women's relation to the economy was always of concern, it was overwhelmingly *ideologies* – of femininity, of wifehood and motherhood – and the influence of these in all spheres which were the focus of feminist scrutiny and attack. This insistence on the determining nature of the ideological contained two elements: it implied a recognition, on the one hand, of the power and persistence of ideologies which justified the subordination of women; and on the other, of the strength of ideas as a motor of change. As a theoretical proposition, it produced reverberations that extended beyond feminism to influence developments within Left social theory over the following decade.

The weakness of the feminist emphasis on ideology as the source of women's oppression was that it probably obscured the substantial material benefits which accrued to men as a consequence of their position within the family. Theoretical attention to this came much later. During the early period, the concept of male supremacy and chauvinism was certainly present in the political rhetoric as well as in small group discussions.

Yet, at a more analytical level, the matter was either undiscussed, or men, too, were perceived as victims of the ideologies of masculinity and femininity.

Children and Mothering

As has already been indicated, the aspect of the nuclear family which received most consistent attention in the early texts, and was considered by most feminists of the period as absolutely central to any analysis of the position of women, was the socialization of children. Within this general area, ideologies of motherhood and child-care were subjected to the most historically specific, detailed and frequent criticism. The particular focus was almost always Bowlby's theory of maternal deprivation.[27] First postulated during the 1940s and widely popularized during the 1950s, it suggested that the separation of young children from their mothers, even for relatively short periods, could result in permanent damage and delinquency. Although Bowlby's hypothesis had been subjected to considerable academic criticism, mainly because his studies were conducted on children in institutions, and he himself had withdrawn certain arguments and qualified others, it was not until the feminist onslaught that the pervasiveness of the ideology at a popular level started to decline. Dr Spock rewrote sections of his celebrated baby manual,[28] initially one of the greatest culprits in this process of popularization, in response to feminist pressure. Within a few years, the issue had ceased to be of significance in most feminist discussions of the family.[29] Yet in the initial stages there is no doubt that it was crucial. Several of the texts argued that, in the post-war period, the ideology of maternal deprivation had operated to justify the closure of nursery schools and the exclusion of women from the labour market. They also pointed out that women who stayed at home to look after their babies were, in addition, available to carry

out the important job of unpaid cook and housekeeper for their
husbands and school-age children – workers and future workers.
Thus present in an embryonic form was an understanding of
women's contribution to the reproduction of the labour force, a
perspective which was developed and became dominant among
Marxist feminists later on in the 1970s.[30] What is interesting is
that these conclusions were originally arrived at through an
examination of the 'myth of motherhood' and *not* through an
analysis of the reproduction of the relations of production.

The argument continued by suggesting that the effects of
the 'myth' were not only to confine women to the tedium and
isolation of the home, but also to curtail their activities in all
other spheres. As a consequence of this exclusion, many women
(as well as men) 'glorified' the role of wife and mother. Fur-
thermore, the 'myth' was perpetuated within the family, since
this was the primary site for the socialization of children into
their gender roles; and boys and girls, it was argued, patterned
their behaviour on the parent of the same sex, thus assuring a
continuation of women's subordinate role.

By about 1973, the ideologies of motherhood and child-care
had lost the centrality they had held in the early texts. Since
then there has been little theoretical discussion of these issues.
This is not only because the critiques were so forcefully made
in the initial stages. It is also because an intellectual pursuit of
the issues encounters political dilemmas: they do not always
lead in the right direction; they are not completely subsumable
within the feminist framework. Thus, although the early critiques of Bowlby were absolutely correct in pointing out the
absurdity of assuming that only mothers could care adequately
for children, this was primarily an assertion about the interests
of mothers. The interests of children, their dependency and
vulnerability, have never really been explored within *feminist*
theory. Various related explanations for this are possible: there
are the political fears that too much concern about the needs of

children could feed into the anti-feminist backlash; at a personal level, the issue might be too contradictory to face; finally, a satisfactory feminist theory of children's needs may simply not be possible. Where the question has been addressed, the tendency has been to designate the work non-feminist, in that women's interests are not given priority.[31]

Another prominent feature of the early texts which remained relatively unexamined after the initial years, yet which, in contrast to the previous issue, might well yield more to feminist investigation, is 'the glorification of motherhood'. That is to say, the insistence of many women (outside the movement) that family life and motherhood can be both rewarding and a source of authority. This phenomenon has tended to be constructed as 'false consciousness', an inability to recognize the real nature of oppression. And although some of the early texts touched on the complex nature of the attachment of women to the home – for example, 'Some women resent their husbands' increased participation in the home and see it as an intrusion into the one area where previously they held some autonomy'[32] – it has perhaps been felt that a proper examination of this area would also add grist to the anti-feminist mill. In fact, I think that the feminist failure to look sensitively at traditional (though, of course, highly contradictory) sites of women's power, like the family[33] and physical attractiveness,[34] has proved a theoretical and political error. Theoretically, the failure emerges from the perspectives which view the family as a unit that is wholly bad for women, and women's physical adornment as invariably part of their objectification. Politically, this insensitivity might well have curtailed the expansion of the movement.

Totally absent from the early writing was any discussion of youth as a category within the family, and the complex interaction between gender and generational relations. The emphasis in youth studies was on boys and street culture.[35] It is only in the last few years that attention has been focused on adolescent girls, and on the specificities of the regulation of young people within the domestic sphere as well as on the street.[36]

This absence of attention to adolescence within the family also highlights another gap. The early texts focused exclusively on the domestic as a context of care for very young children (probably a reflection of the authors' personal circumstances). The periodicity of family life was not taken into account: but children grow and have changing needs, they become increasingly capable of making practical, emotional and financial contributions. The difficulty of establishing the point at which the fulfilment of children's needs amounts to exploitation of adult (maternal) labour, and the nature of this, has barely been touched on in feminist theory.[37]

The Economy

The issue of domestic labour was categorized both under 'wifehood/motherhood' and 'the economy of the family'. Most often in the early texts it was subsumed under the former. Juliet Mitchell, for example, although drawing attention to the material value of housework, does not include it as a significant component of any of her four structures (production, reproduction, socialization and sexuality). It was the *experience* of housework that tended to be emphasized, its triviality and privatization.

Those accounts which situated domestic labour in the economy derived mainly from socialist women who were not prepared to relinquish the primacy of the economic in determining women's position. For example Margaret Benston in Canada in 1969[38] argued that housework was a pre-capitalist form of production, it constituted the economic base of women's subordinate status; women were not only discriminated against but exploited; unpaid labour in the home contributed to the profits of capitalists. Jean Gardiner, in a paper entitled 'The Economic Roots of Women's Liberation', given at an International Socialist women's conference in 1970, argued that: 'The labour of the worker and his wife is appropriated, the one directly and the other indirectly, by capital.'[39] These were the earliest attempts to construct a Marxist analysis of the value of housework and its relation to capitalism. The objective was to fill in the gaps in Marxist theory and also to force the issue of women on to the socialist agenda. The work culminated in the mid 1970s in what has become known as the domestic labour debate.[40]

Some of these ideas penetrated the family critiques that emanated from within the early women's liberation movement, but were not characteristic of them. For example, Sue Sharpe addresses the question of the value of women's labour to capitalism but concentrates predominantly on how this was expressed at the level of ideology. Sharpe also proposes that the family constitutes a 'subordinate mode of production', though without specifying what this means. Whether the family was a 'pre-capitalist' or 'subordinate' mode of production, or whether it was merely characterized by 'different relations of production', also became a major issue in the domestic labour debate.

A quite different materialist approach to these questions was demonstrated in Christine Delphy's pamphlet, *The Main Enemy*,[41] which was published in France in 1970, though not translated into English until 1977. In it, Delphy argues that the family constitutes a *distinct* mode of production, which co-exists with capitalism, in which the labour of women is appropriated by *men*; the emphasis is on relations of exploitation *within* the unit of the family. Delphy's analysis undoubtedly continued to have theoretical reverberations for longer than any other text of the early period. It formed a major plank in the debates about the relationship between capitalism and patriarchy which were to preoccupy feminist theorists at the end of the 1970s. The reason her work was both so influential and contentious was because she insisted on focusing on the benefits of women's unpaid labour which accrue to men rather than capital.[42]

In the early British texts, however, discussions of the family and the economy concentrated, on the whole, on the contribution to capitalism made by the family as a unit of consumption. Within this women were the principal agency:

Aspirations to accumulate such commodities as televisions . . . cars etc. are repeated in every single family, providing the immense consumer market necessary for [capitalist] production. Advertising gives the poor housewife the full works . . .[43]

The assertions about the importance of the family as a unit of consumption were relatively unsubstantiated at the time, and as a theoretical avenue this has remained largely unexplored. Yet as Michèle Barrett[44] has recently suggested, this approach might very well prove more fruitful in demonstrating the support of capitalists for a particular family form than either the domestic labour debate or the reproduction of the labour force theories. An examination of one further 'economic' feature of the family – the unequal distribution and control over the wage and commodities (including food) within the family – was not to emerge until later, and has recently produced some very interesting research.[45]

Reproduction and Sexuality

Reproduction and sexuality are the remaining spheres of significance in the early critiques at which I want to look. These were both accorded a wider range of theoretical interpretations (as was the economy) than child-care and motherhood, over which there was considerable uniformity.

For Shulamith Firestone, reproduction constituted the crucial as well as indisputable biological difference between men and women. It formed the material basis for the subordination of women. Only through the development of artificial reproduction would the oppression of women and the biological family end. Firestone's theory tends towards technological as well as biological reductionism. As Rosalind Delmar has pointed out: 'There is no reason why within present institutions, [reproductive] technology should not be used as a further instrument of women's oppression.'[46] This aspect of Firestone's work is more a feat of the imagination than an analysis which offers guidelines for the development of political strategy.

Reproduction was identified by Juliet Mitchell as one of her four structures of women's oppression. She points out that reproduction, sexuality and socialization, all located in the family, are historically and not intrinsically related. The twentieth-century decline in the importance of the reproduction of children is accompanied by the increasing importance of their socialization. These observations formed the cornerstone of her theory, in that she argued that modification in one structure was likely to be offset by reinforcement in another. Thus what was required was a simultaneous transformation of all four structures – what Mitchell, after Althusser, calls a *unité de rupture*. This theoretical assertion was characteristic of the unitary view of the family and women's oppression to which I referred at the beginning of this section. Its implications are anti-reform: improvements in one structure are likely to be cancelled out by renewed disadvantage in another. This is a hydraulic model reminiscent of Reich and (some would argue) Freud, in that it suggests a fixed amount of oppression circulating in the body politic: push it from the hands and it will reappear in the feet. More recent work sees the family as a site on which material, legal, ideological and psychological discourses intersect, but between which there is no necessary correspondence.[47] Thus, for example, changes in family law have no predetermined effects upon, say, ideologies of child-care.

Interestingly, the issues of reproduction and control over fertility were quite often neglected in the early feminist discussions of the family.[48] In the first years of the movement, 'free contraception and abortion on demand' was a major slogan and area of struggle, but on the whole it was defined as a battle between women and the law and the medical profession, rather than one which concerned patriarchal authority within the family. New perspectives on this were developed towards the end of the 1970s: 'The characteristic relation of human reproduction is patriarchy, that is, the control of women, especially their sexuality and fertility, by men.'[49] The problem then became one of specifying the different forms of this control and their relation to production.

Sexuality in the early critiques remained overwhelmingly influenced by the theoretical assumptions of libertarianism. In these, sexuality was constructed as a drive. Its repression created the submissive personalities required by capitalism. (Subsequent contributions rejected the biologistic assumptions of this early work and stressed the social construction of sexuality.)[50] What was added to the libertarian approach by the early women's liberation movement was a signalling of the contradictions between the demand for sexual freedom for all and the continuing double standard by which women were condemned if they exercised this 'freedom' as freely as men. (Or, indeed, if they chose not to exercise it at all.) It was pointed out that the ideology of monogamous marriage applied, in effect, to women only. In this framework, it was considered that the natural sexuality of children was also subjected to repression and should be allowed free expression.

But the critique was not confined to inequalities in degrees of freedom. It was pointed out that the very nature of female sexuality had been defined in terms which suited the desire and pleasure of men. The notion (based largely on Freud) that vaginal and clitoral orgasms were distinct, and that sexually and emotionally 'mature' women experienced the former, was revealed as mythology by the clinical research conducted in the United States by Masters and Johnson. Koedt, in 1969, was probably the first to incorporate this into a feminist analysis.[51] Thus the clitoris as *the* source of the female orgasm was established as a major political issue by feminists from the very beginning of the new wave.

In many of the early discussions of sexuality, pleasure was not related to the 'nuclear' family form, though Pat Whiting examines married women's (lack of) experience of it.[52] Although her general perspective remains within the 1960s' tradition, with its emphasis on the 'liberation' of sexuality, unlike others she does address the issue of lesbianism as an alternative to oppressive and unpleasurable heterosexual relations:

More women [who were previously married] are taking the gay position believing that equality can only be worked out by two similar partners. These women . . . state quite categorically that the male is not necessary for women's complete sexual satisfaction and happiness.[53]

Whiting was more prepared than most writers of the period to perceive sexuality as a political arena of contestation between women and men, and not merely as a phenomenon which had to be liberated from moral and political constraints deriving from tradition and the political and economic organization of society, that is to say, from *beyond* the family.

Some Other Developments

In this evaluation of the early contributions on the family, I have indicated the direction of subsequent work where this developed directly out of the earlier propositions. A number of significant approaches of the 1970s hardly appeared, even in embryonic form, in the early critiques and therefore have not been mentioned. I shall refer to them briefly.

Although the organization of claimants' unions and resistance to the transparent sexism of social security policy towards cohabiting women formed an integral part of early women's liberation movement politics, the part played by state policy in reinforcing a specific family form was examined in detail only later in the 1970s. Hilary Land pointed out that: 'The British social security system, by perpetuating inegalitarian relationships, is a means of reinforcing, rather than compensating for, economic inequalities.' [54] And Elizabeth Wilson looked at the way in which ideologies of femininity and the family influenced social welfare policies, and how these in turn amounted to 'no less than the state organization of domestic life'. [55]

The 1970s also saw a considerable amount of research into historical variations in familial ideologies. [56] Other writers drew attention to the importance of distinguishing between familial ideology and current 'household form' which only infrequently resembled the breadwinning father and dependent mother and children of the ideal typical nuclear family. [57] Several authors wrote about the very substantial violence perpetrated by men against women (and children) within the family, though interpretations of this phenomenon, and of what the appropriate strategy to overcome it should be, varied. [58]

In 1974, Juliet Mitchell argued for a more complex understanding of the child's acquisition of femininity and masculinity within the nexus of familial relations. She was the first to reassert the value of Freud, and in particular his theory of the unconscious, for feminism. [59] Nancy Chodorow, in the United States, also addressed herself to this problematic. [60] She differs from Mitchell in that her explanation for the construction of masculinity and femininity lies in the *social* arrangements of child-care, in which women mother (and thus make it amenable to change), rather than in the universal nature of the Oedipal conflict. Almost invariably, it is women with whom young children form primary emotional bonds and from whom they must

separate as they mature. It is this asymmetrical early environment which determines personality differences between men
and women, and women's subordinate status. Chodorow's
argument implies that the key to rupturing existing gender
relations lies in the creation of new patterns of parenting in
which men participate equally.[61]

Probably the most significant theoretical project with a bearing on the family was the attempt, in the late 1970s, to establish
a definition of patriarchy and its relation to capitalism. This
was a highly complex debate which, to simplify it grossly, was
about whether the oppression of women was determined primarily by their relation to capitalism or to men. Patriarchy
remained a relatively descriptive concept which was employed
in a variety of ways to refer to the subordination of women as a
category in relation to men. Because some early radical feminists
used it to designate a social division between men and women
both more deep-rooted and more influential than the division
between classes in capitalist society, it was on the whole rejected
by Marxist and socialist feminists. This is not to say that Marxist and socialist feminists remained uncritical of the failure of
Marxism to examine the specificity of women's position. They
were, however, unwilling to take on an explanation for the
subordination of women that could not ultimately be incorpor-
ated within a Marxist framework, which (at its crudest) posits
that all aspects of the social totality are in the last instance
determined by the capitalist mode of production. In this kind
of analysis, the sexual division of labour in the family and
discriminatory state legislation, for example, were explained in
terms of their relation to capitalism; the benefits for men tended
to be ignored.

Significant among the critics of this kind of perspective were
Heidi Hartmann in the United States and Christine Delphy in
Europe. Hartmann, who characterized herself as a feminist
socialist, refused to give capitalism priority and insisted that

Marxism was unable to explain the particular oppression of women.[62] This could only be done by reference to gender hierarchy–patriarchy. For Hartmann, patriarchy and capitalism were two distinct systems whose interrelations varied at any given historical moment. Each could determine the other. Delphy's propositions (already referred to in the 'economy' section of this chapter) were not dissimilar to Hartmann's and formed the foundation of the radical feminist position in the British capitalism–patriarchy debate. With Diana Leonard, she argued that the family, as a distinct economic system in which women's labour was exploited by men, co-existed with capitalism but was not internal to it.[63] It was the organization of labour within the family which constituted the material basis – that is to say, the most significant determinant – for women's oppression in other spheres. Because Delphy and Leonard called themselves radical feminists, their analysis was often erroneously confused with those of revolutionary and some other radical feminists (who stressed essential biological differences between men and women, and politically argued for separatism from both men and the Left). This confusion (as well as the influence of orthodox Marxism in Britain) might well have been responsible for the reluctance of Left feminists to consider Delphy's propositions carefully. Hartmann's work was not received as critically by socialists either in the United States or here.

Inevitably, these are highly caricatured representations of the theoretical positions taken up in the debate.[64] Although in my opinion these positions are best imagined situated along a continuum rather than entrenched in opposing camps, there were all the same important differences between those feminists unwilling to relinquish the idea that capitalism was the ultimate beneficiary of women's subordination and those who argued that it was men. In the end, the effect of the debate was probably to draw out more clearly the distinctions between feminists at opposite ends of the continuum.

In the period of the early women's movement, a far less developed theoretical and political polarization had existed.[65] Socialist feminists *did* draw attention to male violence and radical feminists *were* concerned with the exploitation of women in the labour force. As I have already argued, these early feminist theories were, on the whole, developed in conjunction, in order to map out an unexplored terrain. The project was a collective one. Differences between theories can often be accounted for through an examination of the perspectives with which historically they were associated. Thus, in their analyses of women, feminists in the United States were more inclined to establish analogies with caste and race[66] than were feminists in Britain, whose close association with the Left led them to give priority to questions of class and the relationship of women's liberation (a non-class movement) to the working class.[67]

The development of different tendencies within feminism in subsequent years contributed to a greater refinement of the feminist problematic; yet the abrasive theoretical and political encounters between tendencies sometimes forced a retreat into increasingly defensive and abstract positions formed *in opposition* to those of other feminists. Energy was often dissipated within the movement instead of being directed into engagement with the world 'outside'.

3. What Now?

Over the past decade, the family has been broken from its idealized image as a unit and a haven and exposed as a site of domination and exploitation. This has not happened only within the confines of the movement. The ideas generated there have been increasingly disseminated and popularized. There has been a massive output of writing and the establishment of several feminist publishing houses. The feminist magazine *Spare Rib* has an estimated readership of 100,000. Women's magazines as different as *Cosmopolitan* and *Woman's Own* regularly have articles which seriously address feminist issues. These have combined with the impact of activists in teaching, community work and trade unions to the point where feminist ideas have, in many instances, become part of a common-sense way of viewing the world.

Recent theoretical work has tended to move away from the schematic analyses which characterized the capitalism–patriarchy debate of the late 1970s, and has instead concentrated on the specificities and contradictions of femininity and family life. The component parts of women's subordination do not inevitably coalesce to form a coherent whole. Nevertheless, a recognition of these contradictions and of the limitations of voluntarism in our personal lives must not allow us to absolve the domestic sphere from further radical critiques. The Feminist Review Collective has recently urged:

> . . . a return to the analysis of the family and the split between the public and the private as a source of women's (and children's) oppression. Somewhere along the line the challenge to the oppressive family disappeared.[68]

The publication of this book is evidence of a renewed concern with the family as one of the key sites on which womanhood is acted out and perpetuated.

Yet, politically, the specific circumstances of women's lives are often still not taken into account in the formulation of policies, even by the Left. The socialist Alternative Economic Strategy is an example of this, and has therefore been subjected to considerable criticism. This is one of a range of factors which has contributed to a shift in feminist political activism over the last few years. Large numbers of women previously engaged primarily in relatively small-scale and local feminist campaigns have joined the Labour Party. The specification of ideals, the popularization of feminist perspectives, and grass-roots community organization – however important – are no longer considered sufficient. Feminist objectives have expanded to include the formulation of *realizable* strategies for concrete reforms which can ensure a redistribution of resources and new legislation to promote and protect the interests of women.[69] These must be achieved in order to create a base – a precondition – from which to readdress the issues of consciousness and ideology, and redress the balance of power and privilege.

Notes and References

1. For a discussion of these ideas, see L. Segal in this volume, pages 35–7.
2. S. Rowbotham, 'Women's Liberation and the New Politics', in M. Wandor (ed.), *The Body Politic*, Stage 1, 1972.
3. M. Benston, 'The Political Economy of Women's Liberation', *Monthly Review*, September 1969.
4. A. Coote and B. Campbell, *Sweet Freedom: The Struggle for Women's Liberation*, Picador, London, 1982.
5. R. Wortis, 'Child-rearing and Women's Liberation', in Wandor (ed.), *The Body Politic*.
6. ibid., pp. 129–30.
7. J. Williams, H. Twort and A. Bachelli, 'Women in the Family', in ibid.
8. ibid., p. 35.
9. Rowbotham, in ibid., p. 5.
10. Williams, Twort and Bachelli, in ibid., p. 31.
11. See, for example, A. Oakley, *Sex, Gender and Society*, Temple Smith, London, 1972.
12. See, for example, S. Crockford and N. Fromer, 'When is a House not a Home?', in Wandor (ed.), *The Body Politic*.
13. S. Firestone, *The Dialectic of Sex*, Morrow, New York, 1970.
14. ibid., p. 232.
15. ibid., p. 234.
16. In the last few years, the utopian in feminist thought has more often been expressed in fiction. See, for example, M. Piercy, *Woman on the Edge of Time*, Women's Press, London, 1978.
17. W. Clark in this volume (pages 168–89) also discusses some of the difficulties.

18. M. Nava, 'The Family: A Critique of Certain Features', in Wandor (ed.), *The Body Politic*.

19. ibid., p. 43.

20. J. Weeks, *Sex, Politics and Society: The Regulation of Sexuality since 1800*, Longman, London, 1981, and S. O'Sullivan, 'Passionate Beginnings', in *Feminist Review*, 11, 1982, have also cited 1972 as a significant year in this respect.

21. Between 1970 and 1979, the divorce rate trebled for those under twenty-five, and doubled for those over twenty-five. The decade has seen a phenomenal increase in numbers of people who choose to cohabit rather than marry, though precise figures for this are not so easily obtainable.

22. Psychoanalytic theory has more often been used by socialist feminists in order to understand sexuality. See, for example, *Feminist Review*, 11, 1982, and *M/F*, nos. 5 and 6, 1981, though there are also important differences between these two journals.

23. B. Campbell, 'Feminist Sexual Politics', in *Feminist Review*, 5, 1980, p. 18.

24. Juliet Mitchell's *Women's Estate*, Penguin Books, Harmondsworth, 1971, stands head and shoulders above the rest.

25. Mitchell in her analysis in ibid. argues for a 'complex unity of separate structures'.

26. ibid., p. 155.

27. Wortis, 'Child-rearing and Women's Liberation', art. cit.; see also Mitchell, *Woman's Estate*; Nava, 'The Family: A Critique', art. cit.; S. Sharpe, 'The Role of the Nuclear Family in the Oppression of Women', in Wandor (ed.), *The Body Politic*; *Psychology Shrew*, 1972; A. Oakley, *Housewife*, Penguin Books, Harmondsworth, 1976; and many more.

28. B. Spock, *Baby and Childcare*, New English Library, London, 1969.

29. For a further discussion of this, see D. Riley in this volume.

30. For a discussion of this, see S. Himmelweit in this volume.

31. The question of children's interests has been addressed by J. Hodges, 'Children and Parents: Who Chooses?', in *Politics and Power*, vol. 3, Routledge & Kegan Paul, London, 1981.

32. Nava, 'The Family: A Critique', art. cit., p. 39.

33. An exception to this is Valerie Walkerdine's fascinating article, 'Sex, Power and Pedagogics', in *Screen Education*, 38, spring 1981, in which she looks at the way in which small girls in nursery schools are the subject of a variety of contradictory discourses. Within the domestic, they exercise considerable power over small boys.

34. Two recent pieces of feminist journalism indicate a change in this. See E. Fairweather in *Cosmopolitan*, July 1982, and E. Wilson in the *Guardian*, 26 July 1982.

35. For an excellent evaluation of these, see A. McRobbie, 'Settling Accounts with Subcultures: A Feminist Critique', in *Screen Education*, 34, 1980.

36. M. Nava, 'Girls Aren't Really a Problem: So if Youth is not a Unitary Category, What Are the Implications for Youth Work?', in *Schooling and Culture*, 9, 1981. For further discussion, see also A. McRobbie and M. Nava (eds.), *Youth Questions: Gender and Generation*, Macmillan, London (in the press).

37. The exception is Diana Leonard, *Sex and Generation*, Tavistock Publications, London, 1980.

38. Benston, 'The Political Economy of Women's Liberation'.

39. Quoted in Sharpe, 'The Role of the Nuclear Family in the Oppression of Women', art. cit., p. 140.

40. For further discussion of this, see S. Himmelweit in this volume, pp. 108–15.

41. C. Delphy, *The Main Enemy*, WRRC, 1977.

42. For an excellent discussion of these issues, see A. Phillips, 'Marxism and Feminism', in Feminist Anthology Collective (ed.), *No Turning Back*, Women's Press, London, 1981.

43. Sharpe, 'The Role of the Nuclear Family in the Oppression of Women', art. cit., p. 139.

44. M. Barrett, *Women's Oppression Today*, Verso Editions, London, 1980.

45. See, for example, L. Oren, 'The Welfare of Women in Labouring Families 1850–1950', in M. Hartmann and L. Banner (eds.), *Clio's Consciousness Raised*, Harper & Row, London, 1974; H. Land, *Parity Begins at Home*, EOC/SSRC, 1981; A. Whitehead, '"I'm Hungry Mum": The Politics of Domestic Budgeting', in K. Young, C. Wolkowitz and R. McCullagh (eds.), *Of Marriage and the Market*, CSE Books, 1981.

46. R. Delmar, 'What is Feminism?', in Wandor (ed.), *The Body Politic*.

47. An example of this kind of approach is F. Bennett, R. Heys and R. Coward, 'The Limits to Financial and Legal Independence', in *Politics and Power*, vol. 1, Routledge & Kegan Paul, London, 1980. See also J. Donzelot, *The Policing of Families*, Hutchinson, London, 1980.

48. For example, in M. Wandor's collection, *The Body Politic*, it is hardly mentioned in the articles which focus on the family and only really receives attention in the section entitled 'Crime and the Body Politic'(!).

49. M. McIntosh, 'Reproduction and Patriarchy', in *Capital and Class*, 2, 1977, p. 122. See also R. McDonough and R. Harrison, 'Patriarchy and Relations of Production', in A. Kuhn and A. M. Wolpe (eds.), *Feminism and Materialism*, Routledge & Kegan Paul, London, 1978; and F. Edholm, O. Harris and K. Young, 'Conceptualizing Women', *Critique of Anthropology*, 9 and 10, 1977.

50. There are two main approaches within this general category. The first is adopted by writers influenced by Foucault and certain readings of Freud; see the journal *M/F*. The second is influenced by the interactionist perspective of Gagnon and Simon; see S. Jackson, *On the Social Construction of Female Sexuality*, W R R C, 1978.

51. For a more detailed discussion of this, see Campbell, 'Feminist Sexual Politics', art. cit.

52. P. Whiting, 'Female Sexuality: Its Political Implications', in Wandor (ed.), *The Body Politic*.

53. ibid., p. 212.

54. H. Land, 'Women: Supporters or Supported?', in D. Leonard Barker and S. Allen (eds.), *Sexual Divisions in Society*, Tavistock Publications, London 1976, p. 108.

55. E. Wilson, *Women and the Welfare State*, Tavistock Publications, London, 1977. M. David, *The State, the Family and Education*, Routledge & Kegan Paul, London, 1980, has also addressed these issues.

56. See, for example, C. Hall, 'The Early Formation of Victorian Domestic Ideology', in S. Burman (ed.), *Fit Work for Women*, Croom Helm, London, 1979; and L. Davidoff, J. L'Esperance and H. Newby, 'Landscape with Figures', in J. Mitchell and A. Oakley (eds.), *The Rights and Wrongs of Women*, Penguin Books, Harmondsworth, 1976.

57. M. McIntosh, 'The State and the Oppression of Women', in Kuhn and Wolper (eds.), *Feminism and Materialism*; Barrett, *Women's Oppression Today*.

58. See E. Pizzey, *Scream Quietly or the Neighbours Will Hear*, Penguin Books, Harmondsworth, 1974; J. Hanmer, 'Community Action, Women's Aid and The Women's Liberation Movement', and A. Weir, 'Battered Women: Some Perspectives and Problems', in M. Mayo (ed.), *Women in the Community*, Routledge & Kegan Paul, London, 1977; and J. Radford, 'Marriage Licence or Licence to Kill?', in *Feminist Review*, 11, 1982.

59. J. Mitchell, *Psychoanalysis and Feminism*, Penguin Books, Harmondsworth, 1975.

60. N. Chodorow, *The Reproduction of Mothering*, University of California Press, 1978.

61. For a further discussion of these points, see M. Barrett and M. McIntosh, *The Anti-Social Family*, Verso Editions, London, 1982.

62. H. Hartmann, *The Unhappy Marriage of Marxism and Feminism*, Pluto Press, London, 1981.

63. C. Delphy and D. Leonard, *Women and the Family*, Tavistock Publications, London (in the press).

64. See Phillips, 'Marxism and Feminism', art. cit., and V. Beechey, 'On Patriarchy', in *Feminist Review*, 3, 1979, for detailed discussions of the positions which were taken up.
65. Despite Mitchell's schematization in *Women's Estate*.
66. R. Dunbar, 'Female Revolution as the Basis for Social Revolution', in R. Morgan (ed.), *Sisterhood is Powerful*, Vintage, New York, 1970.
67. A. Bachelli, R. Delmar, A. Hodgkin, I. Matthis, L. Merrington, J. Mitchell, M. Rothenburg, J. Stern, H. Twort and J. Williams, 'Women's Liberation', in *Black Dwarf*, 5 September 1970.
68. Feminist Review Collective, *Feminism and the Political Crisis of the Eighties*, *Feminist Review*, 12, 1982.
69. See final chapter of Coote and Campbell, *Sweet Freedom*, for a detailed discussion of what these could look like.

*

I would like to thank Peter Chalk, Angela McRobbie, Adam Mills, Francis Mulhern and Lynne Segal for their time and helpful comments.

4 Production Rules OK? Waged Work and the Family

SUSAN HIMMELWEIT

The demand of the women's liberation movement which has always gained the most support from women not yet allied with the movement and from progressive men is the one for equal opportunities in employment. It is also the demand on which socialist feminists found their feet. It is here that the disadvantaged position of women is most blatant, and in some ways the rights of individuals most clear. Why should women have to work almost half as long again as men for each pound we earn?[1] Why should we suffer rates of unemployment which have increased more than twice as fast as men's?[2] Why should women be concentrated at the bottom rungs of jobs, even in those occupations, such as primary-school teaching, which are so predominantly female?[3]

Socialists had always been aware of this 'super-exploitation' of women, but few socialist feminists agreed with Engels that the wholesale entry of women into paid employment would solve the problem,[4] for it seemed clear that women's secondary position in paid employment was somehow connected with our primary responsibilities in the home. Whether it was to explain employers' discrimination against married women, unions' unwillingness to fight for equal rights or simply women's own unwillingness to make themselves available for the long hours that men were prepared to stay at work, the answer seemed to lie in the family.

But this posed a problem for socialists and for those of us who grew to feminism through our involvement in Left politics. For the family was not really political; it was just our personal problem. And it was unreasonable, trivial and somewhat distasteful to suggest that changes might be needed there. And this reluctance seemed, too, to have a backing in the theoretical canons of Marxism from which our practice was supposed to grow. For Marx had insisted that the basis of capitalist society, and therefore of its injustices, lay in the exploitation of the working class by capital at the point of production; and that meant during the period for a worker between arriving at and leaving through the factory gates. Everything else was secondary, 'superstructural', to be explained as a result not as a cause of the primary exploitation of the wage-worker by his (usually) capitalist employer. In particular, the specific sort of family in which we lived, the honed-down, nuclear family of modern capitalism, was part of such a secondary superstructure. Indeed, it was usually seen, above all, as one of the important ideological structures of our society, as though what we *thought* about the family and what it made us *think* was the main way in which it was significant.[5]

But there was something logically contradictory in this position. If the family's effects were mainly ideological, why did they seem to be such important determinants of women's position at the point of production? Wasn't the basic tenet of Marxist materialism, that material practices, that is, those around production, are determining of rather than determined by ideological forces? So how then could the ideology of the family be what explained gender divisions at the ever-so-material workplace?

In response to this, socialist feminists set about looking for what was called, somewhat portentously, 'the material basis of sexism'. Its discovery would, it was thought, put feminist struggles on the map, the one being used to chart the strategic assault on capitalism. Accepting that 'material' must have to do with production, we challenged instead the other half of the logical contradiction: that the family was primarily to do with ideology.

The home is just like a factory, argued Selma James and Maria Dalla Costa in 1973.[6] It was on this basis that the campaign for 'Wages for Housework' was launched, which enjoyed significant support from women in the early 1970s in this country, in North America and above all in Italy, where some of its main ideas originated. The argument worked by analogy with the factory owner who makes a profit from the difference between the money paid out to workers as wages and the value added in the process of production. Since, under normal circumstances, products can be sold at a price which more than covers their cost of production, workers are exploited because they are not paid the full value of what they have produced. It is out of this exploitation that profits are made and the capitalist factory and thus the capitalist economy as a whole runs.

James and Dalla Costa argued that what was going on in the home was similar. Housewives produce something needed by the capitalist economy, the ability of the members of their family to work. For workers would not be fed, housed in clean conditions and generally serviced without the domestic labour of housewives. And then there would be no working class for the capitalist class to exploit. Therefore, they argued, the capitalist class made their profits as much from the domestic labour of housewives as from the workers they directly exploited in their own factories. The only difference between the situation of a full-time housewife and her wage-worker husband was that he was paid and she was not, which gave him considerably more power. Wages for housework would therefore solve this basic inequality and give women, through money, the power to press for more far-reaching changes in their lives.

It is easy to see why this campaign won some considerable support, for it is, of course, an appealing idea that we should all have the work we do recognized and paid for. The slogan proved to have a resonance among many women, including some not generally favourable to the women's movement. But against this it was argued that to pay housewives for doing domestic labour would entrench rather than challenge the assumption that housework was women's work, given the way that paid work tended to get segregated into men's and women's work anyway. Housework would simply become the lowest and least desirable of women's work, and attempts either to get men to share in housework or to change the content and relations of housework itself would come to a standstill.[7]

For this, it was argued by those who disagreed, was exactly what was wrong, not only with the demand for wages for housework but also with the argument, by analogy, with wage-work that lay behind it. This argument had concentrated on the *similarities* between wage-work and housework while, if we were really to uncover the material basis of sexism, it was on the *differences* between men's and women's labour that we should focus.[8]

Housework differs from wage-work in all sorts of ways besides being unpaid. At this stage in the debate, we tended to talk as though housework was synonomous with women's work, and wage-work, although also done by women, was the paradigm case of men's work. In other words, we assumed that the primary sexual division of labour in our society is that between domestic labour in the home and paid labour for capital. So, in giving an account of the differences between wage-work and housework, I shall give a flavour of the debates of the time by referring to a wage-worker always as 'he' and those engaged in domestic work as 'she'. Of course, this is inaccurate, above all, in the first choice of pronoun, since most housewives do at least part-time wage-work as well, but I shall return to the significance of this rather inadequate convention later.

A wage-worker for a firm works because 'he' is paid a wage. So he sells his ability to labour for definite periods of time which are agreed with his capitalist employer. The rest of his time is his own and so there is a clear separation in his life between work and leisure. And he spends his wages on things which he consumes away from his place of work, so production and consumption are two clearly distinct activities in his life, separated both emotionally and physically. The work itself, a rigidly timed necessity, goes on at the workplace together with workmates similarly exploited by capital, with whom friendship may or may not develop. Consumption, on the other hand, is part of leisure and goes on in or around the home, largely with other members of his family or friends of his own choosing. During the time he is working, he is told what to do by his employer or his manager who controls the labour process, decides who does what, employing people of various skills as needed, all of whom work together to produce the final product. But the housewife who is not paid a wage has a quite different reason for the labour she performs. The reason she works is so that her family can consume the products of her labour, so that they have cooked meals to eat, clean clothes to wear and a tidy house to live in. But there is no rigid separation in her life between work and leisure. For the housewife, the home is her place of work but she has nowhere else provided for her leisure. Also, because she is not paid for her work, there is no employer to pay her more or less according to how many hours she has worked, and so the amount she spends on getting the housework done is not subject to negotiation. She is in control of her day-to-day pattern of work, organizing her own time to fit in with the demands of the rest of her family, though the overall control of the standards of her work is set by the expectations of a comfortable family life, expectations which are not purely individual but reflect societal norms transmitted by, for example, women's magazines, state agencies or the disapproval of mothers-in-law. There is little division of labour in housework: one person does nearly all except a few clearly specified tasks which change over time. Men may now bath the baby sometimes, or children help with the washing up, but overall responsibility remains Mum's. And there is practically no cooperation; all housewives do roughly the same type of work and they do it in isolation. A few activities, such as shopping, do bring housewives into contact with each other, but this is not to divide out the labour. It is simply a number of people involved in doing the same activity in parallel.

So one of the major differences between wage-work and housework is about how control is exercised. A wage-worker is told what to do by his employer, but behind this control lies another disciplining force, the need to make profits. This becomes a unifying, controlling force on all wage-workers, however understanding and benevolent their own particular employer might be. And it is this need to make profits which makes capitalist production very dynamic, constantly subject to change as new methods are found and new skills developed in order to produce products more cheaply and profitably.

But a housewife has no employer standing over her making sure her labour is as efficient as the next woman's. Change, when it happens, tends to come from outside: washing machines and frozen food become available or the local nursery is closed down. There are, of course, plenty of ideological pressures to conform to the accepted standards of the day and women's magazines are one of the most successful purveyors of such images of the competent housewife. But these pressures, though just as real, are different from those on a wage-worker. This is because her 'contract of employment' is not an exchange contract and cannot be reduced to a simple cash transaction, with the specific disciplining force that the need to make profits imposes. The 'contract' under which a housewife works involves emotional ties and economic dependence of a far more wide-ranging and less specified nature, whether it be formalized in a marriage contract or is just a 'labour of love'.

But it is not only a housewife's labour time that is not

regulated by an exchange contract. Because the products of her labour are not sold but are consumed directly by members of her family, they do not enter into the general distribution process and so go unrecognized by the rest of society (and, so often, by the members of her family). Government statistics ignore them; housework does not figure in the statistics for Gross National Product or any of the other measures used for assessing the growth of the economy. Full-time housewives, if they enter the statistics at all, enter among the unemployed, irrespective of how much work they are doing in the home. In the current recession, for example, little attention has been given to whether the growing amount of official unemployment also results in an increase in the amount of work to be done in the home.

Indeed, the growth of unemployment begs an interesting question as to whether the trend for married women to enter paid labour and use some of the money earned to provide replacements for their own domestic labour can be reversed. Clearly, these women can lose their jobs, and as we have seen, this is happening to an increasing extent, especially to those women who work part-time and do not enjoy the legal protection or the right to redundancy pay, to which those who work more than sixteen hours a week are entitled. But do they now instead do more domestic labour, or does the standard of living of their families just suffer? Has the two-income family become so much the norm that ideological appeals to women not to take men's jobs, as though those were the jobs they had anyway, will have no effect and women will resist redundancy and feel themselves to be unemployed as much as their husbands?

The invisibility of housework in the official statistics is not all that unreasonable, because it does reflect a very real division in a capitalist economy between work whose products become part of the social process of distribution and those which are privately produced, distributed and consumed. Under capitalism, those products produced for sale can be produced by one group of people, the workers employed in a particular capitalist firm, and eventually be used up by another group, consumers for consumption goods or another set of workers for means of production, completely unknown to the producers. The market, that is, the exchange process of buying and selling, carries out this distribution in a completely impersonal way. No capitalist is or has to be concerned about *who* will consume the products, the sale of which will provide his profits. The only important consideration is that the product will sell and at a price high enough to provide the profit which is the sole motivation for entering production at all. In that sense, capitalist firms are there not to produce products but to produce profits. Producing a product is just the means to producing profits and it matters not which products they are, nor who consumes them, nor, provided they go on buying, whether the eventual consumers are satisfied by or benefit from their consumption. This means that capitalist production and the work that goes into it is measured in the market against one scale and one scale only: that of profitability. The money that the sale of a product can make and the statistics that government statisticians collect reflect this; they measure production by the money for which products can be sold and work by the money that has to be paid to get it done.

On this basis, housework does not figure at all. Government statisticians are not in that sense wrong to ignore housework. They are simply reflecting the very real differences which exist between wage-work, whose products are socially distributed through the market, and housework, whose products do not get any further than the housewife's own family. She is, indeed, extremely concerned as to who consumes the products of her labour, what she produces for them and the satisfaction and benefit they get as a result. That her labour is private makes it into a personal service, with the benefits in terms of caring about its effects that this can bring but also the disadvantages of subordinating herself to those members of the family whose labour is recognized as real work by the capitalist market. And there are benefits and disadvantages in the two forms of control we have examined for the wage-workers and the housewife. On the one hand, the housewife does have more control in the daily routine of her life, but the very lack of outside control, of clear hours of work, can mean that she works long hours and ends up unable to stop working because the distinction between labour and leisure is not marked in any way in her life. A 'labour of love' is all very well, so long as it is recognized and does not go on for ever. For the reasons we have seen, in capitalist society divided into two kinds of labour, neither of these conditions are likely to be met, and the following 'Epitaph for a Tired Housewife' is very appropriate:

> Here lies a poor woman who always was tired
> She lived in a house where help was not hired.
> Her last words on earth were, 'dear friend, I am going
> Where washing ain't done, nor sweeping, nor sewing;
> But everything there is exact to my wishes,
> For where they don't eat there's not washing of dishes.
> I'll be where loud anthems will always be ringing:
> But, having no voice I'll be clear of the singing:
> Don't mourn for me now, don't mourn for me never;
> I'm going to do nothing for ever and ever.' [9]

And the separation which arises from the two types of work involved in paid work and housework affects the way we all experience our lives. We live in a society divided into its public and its private spheres. The public world is visible, controlled and powerful, in which only certain forms of behaviour are acceptable. The private world of the family is supposed to be a retreat from that control in which we can let our emotionality rip, with all the beneficial or disastrous consequences this can have for the individuals concerned. And while men identify with the public world, and for them the home is, or they feel should be, a retreat, for women the relation between the two is more complicated. For women are supposed to be the providers of the comfort, both material and emotional, that the home provides, yet they have no other place within which to look for support.

Perhaps this is why the incidence of mental illness is higher among married women than single, while for men it is the other way round. Perhaps, too, this is why women seem to be much more in the forefront of exploring alternatives to the family. In the traditional family, a man's life is structured around and includes two parts: public and private. A housewife's does not. A household, indeed, is not a home without a woman in it, yet the man's presence, while completing our picture of the ideal family, is not essential to it.

So how did this division grow up and how did women get so identified with the home, and the caring emotional values which it is supposed to provide? In this country at least, the pre-capitalist household does not seem to have been a haven of sexual equality. There was clearly men's work and women's work within it, and fathers were the heads of household, organizing the labour of the other members of their family and usually responsible for the purchase of raw materials and the sale of products.

As Miranda Chaytor wrote in her detailed study of a village in County Durham in the years around 1600:

Family and household relations were grounded in an unequal division of power between men and women, adults and children, masters and servants, divisions which shaped household size and structure and ties between family and kin.

And:

Household heads in early modern England were held responsible for the discipline and the moral, spiritual and physical welfare of the members of their household; women's greater practical involvement with children (feeding them, clothing them, keeping them clean) was probably equalled by a greater involvement and identification with their needs.[10]

But there was an important difference in that the household itself was clearly recognized to be a unit of production in which all members of the family had their part to play. The finished products were sold directly by the household, everyone's labour had contributed to them. A similar recognition by the market was thus accorded to the husband's and the wife's and indeed children's labour. That some of her labour time was spent on preparing food for the family or on child-care did not involve a woman in a completely different work relation than her husband. They both worked under relations which had something in common with those of housework and something in common with those of wage-work today.

Similar to contemporary housework was the freedom to choose when and in what way to work. There was no capitalist employer standing over the workers, ensuring that maximum profits be extracted in minimum time. Some of the lack of distinction between work and leisure which characterizes a housewife's life today must, I would guess, have been experienced in the pre-capitalist household. But because some of the products of their labour were sold, and sold to provide the necessities of life on which the whole household survived, a consciousness of the interchangeability of time and money, with which a wage-worker today is disciplined, must have been present within such a household.[11] This would have made all members of the family aware of the importance and time-pressure of their work in a way that is largely missing in the life of a full-time housewife today.

The wage-labour system changed all that. For once a worker was taken from his or her home and paid money directly according to the hours worked, that worker's ability to labour became transformed into a commodity directly exchangeable for money, while that of the members of the family remaining in household production were not so accountable. And when wage-work took over as the normal source of a cash income as the direct production of goods for sale by the household died out, the labour which remained in the household lost all connection with the social, public world of money and the accountability and recognition this provided.

But it was not always the man who was taken into wage labour. Indeed, in the initial stages of the Industrial Revolution, based on textiles, the traditional sexual division of labour, in which spinning was women's labour and weaving men's, was completely reversed. As cotton took the place of wool as the predominant raw material of textiles in the eighteenth century, the bottleneck in the production of finished cloth came at the spinning rather than the weaving stage. For the ratio of spinners to weavers needed was roughly three to one: that is, one (male) weaver needed the output of three (female) spinners to keep him occupied. While individual weavers might solve this problem by employing spinsters from neighbouring households, it was clear in which department the benefits of mechanization would prove most profitable. Hargreaves's spinning jenny, although producing a thread only strong enough to be used as weft, increased the productivity of a spinner manifold. The earliest versions of this invention were designed to be used in the home, and while increasing relatively the output of the female members of a household, did not involve any other major shift in work relations. But subsequent larger versions, and the yet more powerful Arkwright's frame and later Crompton's mule, which were water- or steam-powered and produced a thread strong enough to be used as warp, thus dispensing with the need for hand spun thread altogether, required space and an appropriate site, quite apart from the capital to finance their purchase which the household economy would not provide. This led to the spread of the factory system: workshops in which a number of employees were brought together to work machines producing yarn sold not for their own account but that of their capitalist employers.[12]

While the first employees in the spinning factories were women, as the scale of the work increased, operating the machines came to be seen as skilled, heavy work and men took over. Indeed, they often took their families with them, as spinning by mule required assistants to cope with the large number of spindles on each machine and a man would often employ his own wife and children as his assistants, the full wage being paid to him to cover both his own and his assistant labour. The change from the employment of women to that of men in spinning seems to have coincided with the change from the work being simply that of a machine operative to a supervisory and subcontracting role, in which men could transfer the authority they exercised at home over their family into the workplace. This, more than any real difference of skill or strength required, seems to have been crucial in the masculinization of the spinning labour process.

But the creation of spinning as a male preserve was not won without a struggle. Spinners formed craft unions which excluded all but the close male relatives of spinners from even learning the craft. These unions argued against the practice of employers hiring assistants in support of the old system by which the spinner employed his own assistants and were largely successful in their demands. By excluding women, among others, from taking skilled and well-paid jobs, male spinners gained for themselves both a restricted competition in the labour market for their own skill and the right to employ their own wives and children in a relation of subordination.

That such active struggle by the male working class was

necessary to win for themselves the role of breadwinner in the post-Industrial Revolution family can be seen by the reversal which occurred in weaving. Here, what had been men's work within household production, became women's work as soon as it entered the factories. Initially, the mechanization of spinning brought great benefits to the male handloom weavers, whose labour was now much in demand to work up into cloth the yarn being produced by the spinning factories at an unprecedented rate. But the prosperity of the handloom weavers brought un-skilled men, often immigrants to Lancashire, into the trade, breaking down as they came the traditional protections weavers as craftsmen had enjoyed. As the price of woven cloth fell, whole families had to work at this traditionally male craft to keep the family income above starvation level. Inevitably, even-tually power looms were introduced, more slowly than the mechanization of spinning because weaving had already become so degraded. But it was women and children who entered the weaving factories, leaving the men at home on their handlooms, still with the pride and freedom of being their own masters but without the earning power to keep their families or even them-selves, until the power looms finally broke them. For women and children, the transition had taken three stages: from being, first, the practitioners of a separate and needed skill, that of spinning, within their own homes, to being subsidiary workers to the husband in his dying craft but still within the home, to becoming eventually the factory operatives whose employment drove their husbands to destitution. While male pride and independence may initially have kept them out of the factories, by the 1840s it was too late. Work in the weaving mills had become established as work for women and children, who drew wages well below those of the men employed in weaving, but still brought in far more than their husbands and fathers could earn on their handlooms.

But the Industrial Revolution was not only cotton production.

Indeed, it was a revolution precisely because the factory system, the employment of labour for a wage by capital in pursuit of profit, spread from cotton into all forms of manufacturing. Women and children were employed in the early stages of most industries; the terrible conditions in the mines and the mills provide only some of the most heart-rending accounts of conditions which obtained in many industries. Middle-class reformers combined with the organized working class to protest about conditions.[13] While their motives may have been different, they agreed upon the need for 'protective' legislation restricting the hours women and children could work in the mills and banning their employment in mines altogether. There has been some debate among socialist feminists as to why this happened and whose interests were served by this 'protection' of women by their exclusion from certain occupations and restrictions of their participation in others.

That the legislation was in the interests of both the bourgeoisie and the male working class, at least those who were employed, is generally agreed. Although many capitalists argued against the protective legislation at the time on the grounds that they could not continue to make profits on a shorter working day or without the cheaper labour of women and children, this proved not to be the case, as the more far-sighted 'philanthropic' members of their class had seen, because all capitalists within a given industry were subject to the same restrictions. Competitive pressures were lessened, prices could rise and the same profits be made although higher costs were incurred. So the capitalist class did not lose out, and more importantly, they eventually benefited from the increased health of a workforce not worn out by child labour and with wives at home to look after their domestic needs and transmit those domestic virtues which middle-class Victorians held so dear and found so profitable. A man with sole financial responsibility for a dependent family proved to be a more reliable and more easily controlled worker than the casual and unfit labourer of the earlier period.

The male working class gained as well. Their wages rose as they no longer had to face the 'unfair' competition of the cheaper labour of women and children. Those that so benefited from the higher wages could afford to keep a wife at home, and so the homes to which they returned became more comfortable places as they, too, began to adopt the 'middle-class' values of domesticity.

It is over the effects on working-class women that the arguments start. On the one hand, Jane Humphries has argued that the adoption of the 'family wage' system by which a man could expect a wage sufficient to keep a dependent wife and children, benefited women by freeing them from the necessity to earn their own living in the appalling conditions in which men still had to work.[14] Women, at least those who were wives, shared in the increased standard of living brought by the combination of higher male wages and their own domestic labour.

Heidi Hartmann, on the other hand, has argued that the adoption of the family wage system must be seen as the result of an alliance between the capitalist class and the male working class against women; who, by losing the ability to earn their own living, were forced into dependence on men and into subordinate positions within the home, servicing their husbands' needs.[15]

As Michèle Barrett and Mary McIntosh have pointed out,[16] whatever the effects on working-class wives, the family wage system has had disastrous effects on those women without men to support them and has therefore made marriage and domestic labour the only viable choice for most working-class women. And, to return to today, if trade-union and state policy continues to be framed in terms of an expectation that a man should be provided with an income sufficient to support a dependent family, this must undermine arguments for equal pay, which is certainly a necessary if not sufficient condition for removing women's oppression.

So what can we learn for future demands about the family from this excursion into the process by which the modern family form and its domesticity was created? I think the most important point is to recognize that the division that exists today between what goes on in the family and what goes on 'at work' is not an unchangeable one. If that division was created in the past, it can be changed in the future. And in some ways, of course, it is changing, as married women have begun to re-enter the paid labour force in massive numbers since the Second World War and spend some of the extra money earned on paying for substitutes for those services they would have previously provided by domestic labour. Vacuum cleaners, fridges and frozen peas all provide ways of turning what was previously a housewife's labour – sweeping, shopping or cooking – into a commodity produced under conditions of wage-labour and thus shifting the balance of labour overall away from the home to the capitalist workplace. Other shifts have occurred from the home to the state sector, as state welfare provisions have taken over and transformed women's role as providers of health care or education.

But such shifts, while they do free married women to some extent to take paid employment and thus earn some money of their own, have not eradicated divisions between men and women. Women's primary responsibilities in the home reinforce and are reinforced by our secondary status at work. Even if this collection focused on paid employment rather than the family, it would inevitably touch on the topics of most of the chapters in this book, for women's lives continue to be caught between the two. Role reversal is not feasible for all but a very few couples where the woman's earning power can touch that of the man.

So, although earlier in this article I apologized for using 'he' to refer to wage workers and 'she' to those who did domestic labour in the home, there is an underlying accuracy in this usage, even if it does not correspond to the full-time life-styles of all couples today. For although men may be beginning to do just a little more domestic labour, and most married women are by now part of the paid labour force, whether they currently have jobs or are unemployed, the division of the roles itself has only arisen in the context of a gender-divided society. It is not, as we have seen, that the roles of breadwinner and houseperson were there first and men and women then got allocated to

"Over the past ten years, men have increased their participation in household tasks... by six minutes."

"Mercy, it's the revolution and I'm in my bathrobe."

them, but that that division only grew up on the basis of their being specific to men and women respectively. It therefore seems unlikely we could strip them of their sexist content, giving men and women equal opportunities to step into either role or to share both equally, without fundamentally changing the roles and breaking down the division between the two sorts of work: wage-work and housework.

But why should we want to keep open two such limiting

life-styles as alternatives and simply give men and women both more choice as to which straitjacket or which combination of straitjackets to put on? Rather, it would seem altogether preferable, and if difficult, not without some precedent in history, to transform the relations entailed in both sides of the divide to such an extent that the division between the two disappeared.

This was, indeed, Engels's solution to the problem, for he believed that the entry of women into paid employment would ensure that the chores of domestic labour became taken over as part of 'social production', that is, under capitalism, performed by wage-workers employed by capital. Thus all labour, male and female, would be performed as wage labour for capital. It was not, for Engels, an ideal solution, for the transformation of capitalist relations into socialist ones was the next step; but for him capitalism could at least provide the stepping stone to this by removing the divide between domestic labour and wage labour, by turning the former into the latter.

In the early stages of the modern women's movement, although we did not all share Engels's optimism about the extent to which this could be done, we also looked to the 'socialization' of housework as the solution to the oppressed position of women performing it. It now seems to me that this emphasis was a bit misplaced. For it is not the case that the relations of wage-work are, in all respects, more like those that we would want to create under socialism than those of domestic labour. Some of the freedom – in particular, the less rigid time dimension – of domestic labour by which a housewife does not counterpose labour and enjoyment in her life, while it may be making a virtue of necessity for many women today, is precisely what we would hope would be a reality for work under socialism. The famous phrase with which Marx encapsulated his view of communism, 'When labour becomes life's only want,' does capture the desirable side of that lack of distinction between labour and leisure.

But that is not to say that we should be arguing that the relations of domestic labour, any more than those of wage labour, should be the relations of labour under socialism. For domestic labour is isolating and involves the subordination of the domestic labourer to others of her family. Rather we should be attempting to create new relations for all work, in which those of domestic labour and those of wage labour which are the more humanizing are blended, perhaps together with new elements as yet unknown, to the exclusion of those which we know to be exploitative and oppressive.

Similarly, we must be aiming to break down the divide between public and private life, in which, again, it is not chance that men are identified with one sphere and women the other. We are not just after more women entering into public life and more men taking on private responsibilities. We want to break down the division between the two, but not by destroying all aspects of private life. Instead, we want to take the good aspects that we experience of our private lives and spread them around to invade and transform the public arena at the same time as getting public recognition of the political nature of personal relations. The women's movement has been to the fore in breaking down those barriers, in actions ranging from the introduction of new practices for the conduct of non-hierarchical political meetings to the setting up of refuges for battered wives.

Finally, and I think this is the most difficult point to accept, it seems to me that we will not be able to achieve full emancipation of the potential of both sexes without taking on the question of reproduction, and I mean that in the most basic sense of having babies. For all the discussion about why men and women lead such different lives today takes for granted the basic difference between men and women: that women are potential child-bearers while men are not. Visions of a future society have to take this into account, whether it be by eradicating this difference, as Shulamith Firestone suggested, or, more in line with the spirit of this paper, by abolishing the social division between productive and reproductive labour. What exactly that would mean is hard to imagine, but it would ensure that the production of things did not have more social importance than the production of people. This is, of course, to challenge the basic assumption of Marxism with which this paper started: that the fundamental determinants of oppression in any society turn around the relations of production (implicitly of things). It is only if this is challenged that the oppression of women and the exploitation of the working class can be seen as equally significant features of our society, the removal of which requires the recognition that both are based on the predominance of production relations *in our society*, a predominance that is not inevitable. This may be difficult to accept, but it is only by the struggle against predominance of production relations that the struggle for women's liberation and for socialism can have a genuine common goal.

Notes and References

I would like to thank Lynne Segal for the help, support and above all patience that she has shown in ensuring that this paper got off the drawing board and into print. This paper draws heavily on a unit written jointly by Catherine Hall and myself for the Open University course 'The Changing Experience of Women' and I would like to thank Catherine for all I have learnt from her in the process. Neither of the above should be taken necessarily to agree with the views expressed here nor to share any responsibility for the inadequacies of this paper.

1. In 1979, for every £1 earned by a full-time male manual worker, a full-time female manual worker earned on average 73p. See *Department of Employment Gazette*, 1980.
2. Between 1974 and 1981, registered male unemployment increased by approximately 300 per cent, while in the same period, registered female unemployment increased by more than 800 per cent. See *Department of Employment Gazette*, 1981.

3. The joint NUT/Equal Opportunities Report, *Promotion and the Woman Teacher*, 1980, found 59 per cent of teachers in primary and secondary schools were women, but they had only 38 per cent of the headships in these schools.

4. Engels was a little unclear whether he considered this already to have happened. On the one hand, it would become evident only when women and men were 'completely equal before the law' that 'the first premise for the emancipation of women is the reintroduction of the entire female sex into public industry'. See Engels, 'The Origin of the Family, Private Property and the State', in *Marx and Engels, Selected Works*, Lawrence & Wishart, London, 1968, p. 501. On the other hand, this change had already occurred for the proletariat family where 'large-scale industry has transferred the woman from the house to the labour market and the factory, and makes her often enough the breadwinner of the family, and the last remnant of male domination in the proletarian home has lost all foundation'. See ibid., p. 499.

5. Even Juliet Mitchell, who was well aware of the family's economic significance, defends the importance of its ideological function as having more continuity with the pre-capitalist past than its economic function. Her book includes chapters on 'The Ideology of the Family' and 'Psychoanalysis and the Family', but none on the economics of the family. See J. Mitchell, *Women's Estate*, Penguin Books, Harmondsworth, 1971.

6. M. Dalla Costa and S. James, *The Power of Women and the Subversion of the Community*, Falling Wall Press, Bristol, 1973.

7. M. Molyneux, 'Beyond the Domestic Labour Debate', *New Left Review*, 116, 1979.

8. See, for example, J. Gardiner, S. Himmelweit and M. Mackintosh, 'Women's Domestic Labour', *Bulletin of the Conference of Socialist Economist*, vol. IV, No. 2, 1975, reprinted in *On the Political Economy of Women*, CSE Pamphlet, Stage One, 1976, and E. Malos (ed.), *The Politics of Housework*, Allison & Busby, London, 1980.

9. Traditional, quoted in Malos, *The Politics of Housework*.

10. M. Chaytor, 'Household and Kinship: Ryton in the late 16th and early 17th Centuries', *History Workshop*, No. 10, autumn 1980, pp. 50 and 30.

11. Edward Thompson describes the desperate state of the hand-loom weavers as the price of woven cloth fell and the terms on which they could turn their labour time into money became so unfavourable that they could not escape both starvation and exhaustion. See E. P. Thompson, *The Making of the English Working Class*, Penguin Books, Harmondsworth, 1968.

12. See Catherine Hall, 'The Home Turned Upside Down. The Working Class Family in the Textile Industry in the Early Nineteenth Century', in

E. Whitelegg *et al.* (eds.), *The Changing Experience of Women*, Martin Robertson, London (in the press). The discussion of the textile industry draws from this case-study throughout.

13. See E. P. Thompson, *The Making of the English Working Class*.

14. J. Humphries, 'Class Struggle and the Persistence of the Working Class Family', *Cambridge Journal of Economics*, vol. 1, No. 3, 1977.

15. H. Hartmann, 'The Unhappy Marriage of Marxism and Feminism: Towards a More Progressive Union', *Capital and Class*, No. 8, 1979, reprinted with replies in L. Sargent (ed.), *Capital and Class*, Pluto Press, London, 1981.

16. M. Barrett and M. McIntosh, ' "The Family Wage", Some Problems for Socialists and Feminists', *Capital and Class*, No. 11, 1980, reprinted in a shortened version in Whitelegg *et al.* (eds.), *The Changing Experience of Women*.

5 'The Serious Burdens of Love?' Some Questions on Child-care, Feminism and Socialism

DENISE RILEY

I

Sometimes it seems absurdly daring to go on speaking out, in all this bleakness and poverty, for choice, flexibility, humanity in the having of and the care of children. Campaigns for more and better state child-care continue in the face of cuts by central government on capital expenditure for nursery building, and by local authorities on upkeep. Is this persistence in campaigning a quixotic refusal to face economic realities? These feminist and socialist virtues cost money, whatever else. Where there is no money, or where the distribution of funds is controlled by a different ethic, a different understanding of needs, then child-care sinks to the bottom of the list. There is not even the embittered grim consolation of ascribing this neglect to the hardness of a calculating capitalism, which we shall see pass away into a more generous socialist dawn. It is not merely a problem of Thatcherism coating a false image of the family with marshmallow tones, while at the same time it acts mean-spiritedly. That is there. But there is no automatic opposite – a socialism of abundance which would pay full and imaginative attention to the needs of women with children; plenty does not spontaneously flow from a new socialist order, any more than refusing public welfare provision is a timeless characteristic of capitalism. Political conservatism, in the narrowest sense of 'political', and conservatism of the spirit may frequently run together, but they need not absolutely do so.

A few years ago, it seems many years ago, British feminists used to puzzle aloud over the 'contradictions' of welfare capital-

ism, and look to Sweden where some of our aspirations
appeared to be met; but then distance, we reflected, must be
deceiving us, for we knew that the heart of capitalism was set
against the interests of women with children. Now to write that
is to caricature, to reduce those reflections of the mid 1970s.
We never held, as socialist feminists or as feminist socialists,
such unshaken beliefs in the smooth matching of economies –
capitalist or communist – and public virtues and vices. And as
for this 'we', this writing about 'our' history, and suggesting
what 'we' might turn our minds to, there are drawbacks to this
device. It can have an irritatingly parochial ring. Who is being
addressed by that 'we', except for 'others of us'? And why
should anyone not feeling herself implicated in the pronoun
put up with it? It also imposes an unconvincing unity of socialist
feminism, as if this were a single and programmatic doctrine;
whereas, used so generally, it only really acts as a gesture of
distancing from radical feminism, again undefined. Nevertheless, I am going to go on making use, with apologies, of this
risky 'we'. It is very hard to circumvent, since these remarks are
made out of and back to a specific set of concerns about child-
care, voiced by British socialist feminists over the last ten years
and more. They are intended to suggest ways of contemplating
these concerns – although contemplation must be urgent when
both feminism and socialism are so hard-pressed.

But now, as British conservatism behaves like some cartoon
rendering of itself, it is all the more necessary to hold on to the
liveliness of our scepticism about the wills or abilities of any
governments untouched by any feminism to deliver the social
goods. Not that the writing-in of feminist language to social
programmes guarantees everything. To take the obvious example of Russia in 1917; Alexandra Kollontai, as a leading
Bolshevik, effectively amended that fine Leninist slogan, 'Revolution, Electrification, Peace', to include demands for
crêches, communal kitchens, divorce, abortion – demands tem-

porarily realized, despite or more accurately including their sturdily conservative vision of The Mother. Looking back after the Stalinist enthronement of the ideal family as 'the sacred nucleus of triumphant socialism', Trotsky wrote in his *The Revolution Betrayed* that:

You cannot 'abolish' the family; you have to replace it. The actual liberation of women is unrealizable on the basis of generalized want. Experience soon proved this austere truth which Marx had formulated eighty years ago.

Yet it is evident from Trotsky's own account (even if that were all we had to go on) that the reversing of the earlier social aims of the Communist Party cannot be put down to a lack of means, to national devastation through war and 'backwardness' alone. Imaginative poverty cannot, of course, be held to be utterly independent of brutal shortage; the free spirit needs to eat, too. But one strength of feminism is its potential for keeping alive a voice which speaks over and beyond the recognition of practical necessities and austere truths, and which goes on arguing for the reordering of what is to count as need, what social priorities could be – even, if it has to be, in the teeth of what would seem a sensible cutting of coats according to cloth. Especially where much to do with gender is concerned, we suffer from far too much received 'common sense' already, and would suffocate from generating more of it.

But couldn't it be retorted, that now is no time for wayward assertiveness about the imagination; that this line betrays only a disguised and silly nostalgia for a decade ago, of charm only to its faithful survivors? I don't myself believe that this retort would be to the point. I want to plead the need, instead, for feminism and socialism to respond to the 'current crisis' by being both far more impassioned and more analytical about questions of child-care particularly; to throw them more widely open, and to flee from solidifying into new orthodoxies. For everything tempts us into retreating now, and sometimes it looks as if withdrawing from possibly shaky ideological terrain might be better than an undignified scramble, or at best a scorched-earth policy, in the face of rapid conservative advance. And there is no doubt that the ground held by feminism 'as a whole', so far as there has ever been such a creature, has been terribly uncertain. I am going to say that this, though, does not *very much matter*; but only to the extent that we are fully aware of it, and not caught out by surprise and despair. That awareness would mean that we would not be so up against our own uncertainty, and be so liable to hang on doggedly to familiar inadequate repetitions of the current claimants to the feminist socialist 'line'; we would be in the far more gratifying and flattering position of developing or revivifying so many lines that we could run them round whatever unsupple opponents we found. This may sound as if all that is needed to solve problems of the state and child-care, feminism, conservatism and socialism is some self-delighted mental quickness, and, of course, it is not a contest of ideas only which is being fought. None the less, child-care is peculiarly susceptible, as a question, to the opposite risk: the risk of being relegated as an already completely understood set of wants to the practicalities of campaigns; as if theorists chased around in a fine thin air, while dogged workers pushed on in earlier agreed directions.

At the same time, though, as the questions seem hedged in by the dictates of good sense, the possibilities for a feminist understanding of them can look increasingly vulnerable – or, less generously, implausible. There has always been, since the beginnings of the women's liberation movement in Britain, a strong anxiety at work concerning child-care. The desire not to run any risk of confirming the identification of feminism with anti-child, let alone anti-mother sentiment, has uneasily accompanied the refusal of belief in maternal destiny, in the naturalness and inevitability of who does what in the kitchen. We have always been told that feminism is indifferent to the problems of mothers and children; and that charge has not ever been true. We go on saying what we have repeated for years: no, feminists aren't against mothers; we include mothers; we want 'the right to choose' to have as well as not to have children. Engineering for 'choice' does not mean forgetting that the fundamental choices are founded on having money, a room, a job, some help, and also on the liberty to reflect, to analyse. Even though considering the emotion which pulls many towards child-bearing may do little to clarify the nature of its tug, that time to think, to read, to discuss was in itself an important element in all those conditions for 'choice' which lay, massive and monstrous in their intractability, behind the sparse legal options we necessarily had to focus our attentions on. There was the stubborn hanging-on to whatever accidents of 'choice' our lives had thrown in our way; the recognition that defending the 1967 Abortion Act was an inescapable but partial task.

Why, then, has it been such an enduring charge, that feminism has nothing to say to or about women with children? An impression of child-dumping was conveyed, for some, by one of the original four demands of the women's liberation movement: that for 'twenty-four-hour nurseries'. This was, I think, conceived in the wish for some unchallengeable flexibility for mothers, as well as on the principle of going for the maximum possible; but its phrasing has caused some embarrassment. Against that, though, can be set the far greater evidence of extensive feminist work, not only against the myth of 'maternal deprivation' and the rosiness of domestic life, but, for instance, for child benefit to go on being paid to mothers, for better conditions for unsupported mothers, and, critically, for the legal and financial independence of women. Standards of training and pay for nursery workers have not escaped feminists' attention, either; nor have the chances for improvements in what goes on in local authority nurseries. Despite such work, there has not been a single and resonant feminist 'answer' to problems of child-care; there are very good reasons for this silence on something which can't take one 'answer'; but in a period of gross cutbacks in social provision, it can seem as if we had in the past indulged in empty ideological or utopian thinking ourselves. The wish to dissociate ourselves from being considered toughened abandoners of children returns in force. All the apparent weaknesses of the old debates flood back now. Were we perhaps wrong not to have championed childminders more; and was it after all sometimes truly desolate in the local authority nursery? Bedevilled with vacillating between blaming the recession, or a retrograde national consciousness, or the shortcomings of our own earlier analyses, and unsure – not surprisingly – of how to imagine all of these operating together, a 'feminist mother' may well wonder if she can truly exist as that being. In addition to the suspicion that socialist feminism might be mistaken in its aspirations to produce an all-embracing story of the problems of motherhood, that perhaps there will always be something 'in excess' which can't be fully named by the political descriptions available, there is also the vehement appeal of realism.

For, as women's jobs disappear, the chances of combining work and child-care look increasingly slim. Nursery places wither away unless you can plead exceptional circumstances, 'social deprivation', and then you have nothing guaranteed but a waiting list – unless, indeed, you live in one of the counties which has cut away its facilities altogether. So it may seem almost wilful for feminism to go on concentrating on state provision; should not the tactics change with the hardness of the times? It is not just the faltering of earlier hopes about the liberating crannies to be gouged out of the accidents of the Welfare State. Along with the new wry realism is a new emotional tone. There is more weight, hard to describe except impressionistically, on the elements of pleasure, of love in having and caring for children; an insistence that it's not merely a mournful laborious duty. The 'creative' aspects of motherhood are celebrated again, as they often have been, but without incurring the confident feminist derision of recent years. And, in a way, that is quite right; but it is not an interesting or encouraging kind of rightness. It tells us what we already know: that there are passions and surprises bound up with child-care as well as the exhaustion and isolation dwelt on by women's liberation. But it tells us in a debased language which produces a flat sociology of the emotions, and does so at the expense of thought about practical needs. Meanwhile, throughout the drifts of theories, individual solutions are hit upon, or accidents intervene, and children grow. The tiredness of being on your own with young children can mean that you no longer have the stamina or the heart to go to political meetings. But campaigns, fortunately, go on; the National Childcare Campaign is the current central organization.

One sideways comment: the very term 'child-care' has a dispiriting and dutiful heaviness hanging over it which resists attempts to give it glamour or militance alike. It is as short on colour and incisiveness as the business of negotiating the wet kerb with the pushchair; and it has some of the awful blandness of the 'caring' voiced in the language of psychologized social work, and, increasingly, by anyone else wanting to lay claim to possessing a professional humanity. 'Child-care' has the ring of something closed off, finished, which some people – mostly mothers – know all too much about, and from which other people shy prudently away. Like recommendations for anti-sexist behaviour, it makes the private heart sink a bit, while public socialist heads nod a half-automatic assent, as if recognizing, these days, its inevitability. Can we really offer anything more lively and engaging than the good sense and hot dinners advocated by pre-war Fabians? It is uphill work; but beneath the dull surface of child-care there are profound ana-

lytical difficulties and interests; and excitement can be got out
of it. What I want to indicate is the range and the volatility and
the peculiar attractiveness of the questions which child-care can
put to a feminist socialism. And, to repeat, there will not be an
exhaustive canon of answers – but this does not so much matter.

2

One way of considering these questions and these answers is to
look at their life and their transformations in feminist and
socialist work and thought. The effect, though, of looking at
history may be the production of a gloomy sense of there being
little new under the sun, ideologically speaking. To glance back
and discover that many of the anxieties and debates of the
contemporary women's movement have occurred spasmodically
over the last sixty years may give an impression of intimacy
with past politics, but it is one stripped of consolations. Or
where the arguments from the side of feminism or from
women's labour organizations have visibly altered, the final
effects of the actions of central government or local authorities
over child-care provision may well have been the same over a
long span of years; as with the withdrawals, after both world
wars, of nurseries for the children of women war workers. One
outcome of investigating these movements and backtrackings is
the savage evidence of difficulties obstinately recurring, depriv-
ations persisting, official refusals ossifying.

   The speed, too, with which enthusiasms among socialists and
feminists themselves can flicker in and out of being may bring
about cynicism, or mournfulness. Dreams of Soviet Russia as
the ideal of benign communism which would liberate women
through enlightened public child-care repeated themselves for
feminists in the 1920s, the 1930s, and to some extent in the
1940s; although hopes of sexual liberation and of collectivism
did indeed take on different forms over those decades. The
general dream of Russia was superseded in the 1970s by a brief

dream of China. The women's liberation movement looked to the nurseries of the Cultural Revolution; that generation of feminists did not need to have Maoist convictions to be touched by those rows of shining children, any more than their predecessors had needed Stalinism to support their visions. Common to both enthusiasms was a search for the truth of politics lived in another country, and an indifference to the general question of the nature of the state as well as a straightforward lack of information about the nature of those particular states. How to think about child-care – let alone about contraception, abortion, population control – in relation to both central and local governments is a perennial difficulty. For who are nurseries for? If allotted for the good of 'social hygiene', for the children of 'deviant mothers', for the easier flow of a temporarily needed female labour force, for permitting the employment of women who would not be able to survive without, say, monotonous and badly paid work on top of their domestic work – how are these possible conditions of state bestowal of child-care to be understood and, where need be, contested by feminist campaigns? What were – and are – the engagements and interests of various forms of the state in the sexual, maternal, parental actions of its citizens; and should feminism, less systematically committed to analysing states than various socialisms, always take up an oppositional stance?

It has been the question of the education rather than of the care of children which has brought about the adoption of a clearer if simpler 'line' on the state. The women's liberation movement, at its start closer as a whole to libertarian socialism, was sympathetic to the ideals of non-authoritarian, community controlled education advanced by free schools and children's rights groupings. To these aims, the particular feminist theory of anti-sexist learning was added (and whatever the uncertainties of that as a theory, the spreading outside the formal confines of feminism of the idea that boys need not be boys must have been one of the most thoroughly beneficial bits of popularization that feminism has ever managed). This early broadly libertarian leaning of women's liberation was overtaken as campaigns spread, diversified, linked up with other work. Both political and organizational changes of emphases saw a concentration on labour organization; the feminist infiltration of union policies occupied the prominence formerly given to 'community politics'. In the name, often, of the rights of women workers, demands for free access to abortion and the defence of existing if inadequate laws, as well as demands for child-care, were voiced at Trades Union Congress level – and at earlier stages by the Working Women's Charter. The *TUC Charter on Facilities for the Under-Fives*, produced in 1978, embodied many feminist aspirations in its call for 'a comprehensive, mandatory service', to include free nursery centres which local authorities would be statutorily bound to provide, and a reform of child-minding and of nursery staff training schemes. In its guarded attitude to workplace nurseries – 'transferring such responsibilities to the employer would be a reversal of the policies of the whole labour movement for a century or more' – the *TUC Charter*, although too sweeping about the coherence of past policies, had drawn the lessons of the postwar period. Between 1945 and 1948, union politics as well as governmental politics drifted well away from commitments to local authority nurseries for all, leaving it instead up to individual employers; one outcome was that the reputation of childcare outside the home fell, along with ambitions to meet social needs. The vagueness and ambiguity, too, of the 1944 Education Act's wording on whether or not local authorities were obliged to provide nurseries according to local wants was also tacitly referred to in the TUC's General Council's wish to see a clear statutory duty enforced. It is horribly striking that this document, only four years old, should now sound like an impossibly dated utopianism. It recommends the consideration of the pay and conditions of part-time work in order to allow 'flexibility' to parents, instead of being forced into formulating a strategy on part-time and unemployment. It could still debate social need, and make claims for the introduction of 'services which enable parents, especially mothers, to make a free choice – whether to work or to stay at home to look after children'.

What are the needs, and what are the choices now? Over three million officially unemployed, and unnumbered thousands of women, unregistered unemployed, do not make the contemplation of these questions a redundant philosophical luxury. They have a persistent life which is especially vexing for a feminism torn into ideological tatters. To flatly assert the needs of women, children and men is of no help here: such claims only serve to increase the vulnerability of a harried feminism to self-doubting revisions, and drive it back on to the conservatism of common sense, the only familiar ground. Instead of asking, in the name of the latter, whether we had not been wrong in our criticisms of the family, we can ask what needs are; where they come from; and who is attributing what to whom. The clash, for example, between the 'needs' of women for (hypothetically or polemically) sexual expression; or to move in search of work; and the needs of children for (in the same vein) 'security' – is that a real clash? It is a feminist commonplace to mention a conflict of 'interests' between men and women – a commonplace open to well-enough founded attack – and yet it is hard to reconcile this with the supposition that children's and women's needs are, on the contrary, in some automatic harmony.

These difficulties do have resonances for feminist political understanding, and can not be dodged as being trivially philosophical. To do so is to lay open a regressive anarchy of competing political rights and needs – of children, of fathers – all set clamouring for attention against those of mothers. I can only mention this problem here and not pursue it; generalizations will not work. Adults' needs and children's needs are neither necessarily consonant *nor* necessarily incompatible; not everything can be accurately read off from the categories of men, women and children. It is likely to be an increasingly sharp question, though, for feminism, since more 'rights' may be increasingly named and laid claim to by more contestants. Who and what is a 'parent', for instance; is there a genuine democracy of parents, inclined harmoniously over the child? Or instead are there only 'mothers' and 'fathers' who are, because of their different powers, capacities and histories, always irreconcilable? Neither alternative, I think, is right. Meanwhile lives get lived out in some admixture of making-do and fortune over the matter of whose interests and wants are pursued – and with prayerful wishes that our children won't grow up to turn round and reproach us with sacrificing their well-being to our ideological convictions. The feminist mother, that uncertain person, may well tremble at *The Woman Who Did*, Grant Allen's novel of 1895. This is the tale of dashed hopes: a terrible daughter who so burned with frustrated social hopes when she realized her own principled illegitimacy that her high-souled mother had only one means of freeing her for respectable marriage. The mother, the woman who did pursue the logic of her own objections to marriage, cleared the path for the conventional child's ambitions by committing suicide.

3

One of the agonies of Grant Allen's heroine, as she arranged herself for the death which, the novel suggests, lies in wait for those who follow through their moral convictions, might have been self-doubt. Composing the lilies across her breast, she could have pondered the question of fashion. Had her life been lived according to principles merely given to her by the transient accidents of styles, fashions of belief? Refusing marriage as a legal shackling of hearts whose only obligation must be spiritual

– was that a passing piece of nineteenth-century feminist moralism which, when lived, had only succeeded in disturbing the child of free love? Within a year of its first publication in Britain and America, the novel had reached its twenty-fourth impression. If we translate the anxiety it embodies into contemporary terms, it emerges as the question of how we manage to bear the vicissitudes of socialist and feminist ideologies. For it is not just a task of opposing a capitalist ideology always 'out there', but also of deciphering our own changing manners and articles of faith.

This is the difficulty entailed by wondering if there are general and distinct socialist and feminist objectives in the care of children, or a quintessentially feminist set of demands to be made. Perhaps nothing can be said which is not traceable to somewhere else; to humanist or liberal beliefs, or even to some spreading of lay psychoanalysis. What about, say, hopes for community control of child-care – who is the community? Or for the 'socialization' of child-care – what are the connections there with conception? What about contemporary China, which is trying to reduce its birth-rate, attempting to make conception itself subject to community planning? Or do we want to say that to conceive a child is private, but to rear it must be the responsibility of the community – doesn't that, though, suppose other conditions? Why should child-care be the province of non-parents too? For the sake of some social generosity? If there are not distinctive and original arguments emanating from a socialist feminism on these speculations which could not be derived from other, occasionally antithetical, political beliefs, we might worry about the consequences for socialist feminism, feeling ourselves at the mercy of fashions in all their volatility. The weight of the passing of time here can seem outrageous. Two years ago, 'we' adhered firmly to such and such a line; and now 'we', probably a compositionally altered 'we', must instead adhere to another. Not only that, but perhaps there are no

coherent lines anyway to bear very much examination; perhaps
there is only a broken scatter of items from here, colourings
from there.

It does seem to me that this despair is misplaced – or rather,
that its expression need not run to a devastating outcome. There
will be a kind of eclecticism about formulations on child-care.
Political thought always, in a way, comes from somewhere else;
there's a necessary stitched-togetherness at work, even though
the dream of a pure and unique place of ideals is not to be
forgotten in the name of a modest practicable daylight. For,
however much history can demonstrate our lack of originality,
the recognition of that need not entail a resentful surrender to
'common sense'. Nor need it render pointlessly 'theoretical' any
attempts to take up eclecticism into some clearly delineated
feminist ideal, even if all the accidents which have coincided to
generate the latter are fully admitted.

So, on the question of what is the socialist feminist understanding of child-care now, the inescapable glances back at the
determinations of present assumptions do not have to induce
pessimism. They can be cheerfully ironic, perhaps, or puzzled;
or sobered by the complexities of things, which is not the same
as pessimism. There is entertainment to be had, too. Even
the impression that there is nothing new under the sun (and so
the sharpness of the question of how to produce a socialist and
feminist programme which does not merely react to Thatcherism, but possesses some independent dash of originality) –
even that impression can result in relief as well as gloom. You
can derive consolation, for instance, from the free-floating
nature of the attachments of socialisms and feminisms to psychoanalysis and psychology. The consolations lie in the release
from having to suppose that there is something necessarily
congruent between them which has at all costs to be 'worked out';
and also in taking this very supposition of congruence to have a
considerable history and political interest in its own right.

The drifts of both feminist and socialist harnessing or rejection of psychoanalytic theories of child-rearing, in particular, can be scanned to this end. Various feminist persuasions have fought since the 1960s against Freud; or have, through Lacan, espoused Freud; or have been repelled by some facets of Reich and charmed by others; and all this is heavily documented. But studious fascinations with psychoanalysis and its uses for a socialist or a feminist pedagogy well predate contemporary involvements. Indeed, terrible solemnities have long been written and spoken in the name of such a pedagogy, and the old 'philistine' jibes at ideals of self-expression which produce monstrous children – and indeed adults – have their place. More seriously, the history of liberal, socialist, communitarian adoptions of psychoanalysis is illuminating in its very fitfulness, as well as in its intensity. Vera Schmidt, from 1921 on, ran a psychoanalytic nursery in Moscow which became a point for political agitation and defence. Both Sigmund Bernfeld and Wilhelm Reich attempted psychoanalytic education in Vienna in the late 1920s – a city which had seen psychoanalysis on the rates from 1918 onwards, when its council had supported the home for juvenile delinquents directed by August Aichhorn, the author of *Wayward Youth* (1925), to which Freud added a preface. These moments of meetings in capital cities between municipal socialism, or at least liberalism, and educational theories touched by psychoanalysis were not enduring.

But free-thinking pockets of Europe became beacons for British socialism between the wars, although most British experiments in education were privately financed: a psychoanalytic socialism on the rates here was hardly plausible. British feminism of certain persuasions was also close to liberal schooling. Dora Russell ran a school from 1927 onwards, initially with her husband, which followed some of these principles. And the degree of at least intellectual interest among British

socialists and educationalists can be gauged – unless their pub-
lishers had badly misjudged the market – by the huge numbers
of European works which Eden and Cedar Paul translated between 1912 and 1927. These books of Freudian-influenced
pedagogy included *The Elements of Child Protection*, *A New
School in Belgium*, *Love in Children and Its Aberrations* and *Set
the Children Free!* In England, the popular novelist Ethel
Mannin produced a 'plea for freedom' in 1931 entitled *Common-
Sense and the Child*, a rather honeyed socialistic work. A. S.
Neill, as a private progressive, well expresses that blend of
simplified psychoanalytic thinking and environmentalism in his
introduction to this book:

When I have a thief to deal with I know at once that he is symbolically
stealing love . . . Isn't it a terrible thought that Dartmoor is full, not of
natural devils, but of the victims of a wrong education?

4
To save the victims, not only of a 'wrong education' and of
emotional lack, but of more visibly punishing attacks like rickets
and hunger, was the aim of a broad and powerful current of
British socialism well before the First World War. To cure
through intervening in child-rearing and teaching *now*, rather
than wait in the hope of revolution later (however revolution
was construed), was the ambition of many shades of socialists,
Christian socialists, feminists, Fabians, liberals, eugenists, educationalists; in and outside of labour organizations, political
parties, and religious or ethical groupings. All of these ambitions
and campaigns cannot be lumped together as 'philanthropy' in
a dismissive sense; although the narrowest philanthropy did
have its own life. How to heal poverty, what the state might do
to cause or ease it, preoccupied the many socialists and feminists
who worried over the depressed lot of working women and
children in particular.

To take one prominent campaigner: the work of Margaret McMillan offers the most vigorous instance of a Christian socialism concentrated on child-care. A foundation member of the Independent Labour Party in 1893, she worked for the Bradford School Board, campaigning for open-air schools, voice production, school meals. Her publications include a pamphlet on 'correct breathing' for children and several books, among which are *Education Through the Imagination* (1904), *The Child and the State* (1905) and *Labour and Childhood* (1907). After leaving Bradford, she settled in London, agitating successfully for compulsory medical inspection in schools, and becoming LCC member for Deptford. Best known, though, was her nursery work; her Deptford nursery was formally opened in 1921, and the Rachel McMillan Training College, named after her sister, in 1930. What form did her theories of practical socialism in the care of children take? One of her reasons for resigning her presidency of the Nursery Schools Association in 1929 is revealing here – that it did not emphasize what she took to be the necessity of a nine-hour day in nursery schools serving 'slum areas'. The nursery school should, she believed, be an unassailably large and curative institution, to dispense three meals a day, paid for by parents; it would act, too, as a mothers' social centre. Here is her passion for fresh air, health and school size, exemplified in a broadcast she made in 1927 about 'The Nursery School':

At 12.30 three hundred little children are fast asleep in little cots where the sun, the blessed doctor in the sky, who cures rickets, can rest on the sleepers. In winter, of course, they are wrapped warmly in red blankets.

Margaret McMillan's conviction that the best way of altering the damaged lives of 'slum children' was early nursery care sprang from her evolutionary socialism; one also opposed to 'doles' as only sapping the latent enthusiasm of the poor for 'self-development'. Infant schools themselves would, she wrote confidently in her 1926 paper, 'Poverty in the Modern State', make 'class-consciousness' a redundant rhetoric: 'The classes will meet there simply because the upper class girl will train and serve there under the teacher.' Nurseries allowed for social mixing; and observation of the life of infant schools could clarify the vexing question of what ills could be put down to 'wrong nurture' as distinct from heredity, and so be in reach of being cured. Margaret McMillan's lyrical descriptions of the improvements wrought in her nursery children afford extraordinary glimpses of a working socialist eugenics in a benign form; this is also from 'Poverty in the Modern State':

In any other area children who have the same chance would look as they look, and be what they are in a year! They would show the real fibre and pattern of the race, like new-cleaned carpets. A crowd of them in St Paul's, or elsewhere, would give pause to the blackest pessimism. It is not possible to believe today that we fairly *see* each other. For nothing hides so well as poverty, and many are poor.

This diction of 'the race', quite congruent with many socialist and feminist persuasions until as recently as the end of the last war, has been heavily played upon – either instrumentally or with true conviction – in reform work for the care of children. Nurseries have been fought for in what 'we' would take to be deeply conservative or reactionary language. What 'we' would understand to be evidently anti-socialist, anti-feminist sentiments about child-rearing, maternity and the state have been wrapped around results which fit with 'our own' aims; what is to be made of this?

   Look, for another quick example of a contrasting approach, at Anna Martin, writing *The Married Working Woman* in 1911 as a piece of polemic for the National Union of Women's Suffrage Societies. She is concerned to defend the native good sense of working-class mothers, their capacity to 'manage' under the most disheartening circumstances. That free school meals system which has so exercised the imaginations of many social-ists, she wrote, 'excites neither enthusiasm nor gratitude'; for working women were 'sincerely apprehensive of the de-moralization of the men'; indeed, they might get given less housekeeping money as an outcome of such public funding. Medical inspections, for which Margaret McMillan had done battle, only served, Anna Martin claimed, to lay extra burdens on the mother, who must cut her already tight spending on food to buy medicines, with doubtful gain. But give working women the vote, she argued, and their influence would not be bent to what others short-sightedly held to be self-evident socialist ameliorations in their and their children's lives. With things as they actually were, to raise the school-leaving age would only cause dismay in the home at the loss of an income. Keeping children out of pubs by law, another well-meant intervention, would do away with the moderating in-fluence of the presence of mothers on drinking men. And, she wrote firmly in *The Mother and Social Reform* in 1913, those women who themselves drank might at least square up to their husbands' violence, and be more vivid than 'colourless submissive drudges'. Her point was that the working wife and mother suffered from more profound grievances than her middle-class critics had supposed or understood. As a result:

... 'mothering' the children of the poor became almost a fashionable sport ... Grave legislators debate the material of which the baby's nightwear should be composed, and endeavour to lay down the princi-ples which should regulate its sleeping arrangements. Local authorities decide the hours at which Annie may earn two pence by cleaning steps or Johnnie add to the family income by lathering chins.

These benign interferences, said Anna Martin, were, like the machinery of school meals and medical inspections, effec-tive diversions from the political powerlessness of the

unenfranchized working-class women. What was really wanted
was legal redress instead of pieties when husbands wilfully
failed to support the family:

Let her nominal right of maintenance for herself and her children be
transformed into a real one, and it will be found that her supposed
passion for working ten hours a day in a jam factory for a mere
pittance is a figment of men's imagination.

The Labour Party, whose 'leaders wax eloquent over the grievances of the sweated industrial female workers', was notably
silent on the question of the wife and mother in the home. For unlike the woman waged worker, she lacked any guaranteed recom-
pense, however inadequate, for her labour; and she had no means
of protection against the violence of her husband-employer.

So there is Anna Martin, critical, under the banner of the
National Union of Women's Suffrage Societies, of attempts
made in the name of socialism and women's rights to better the
lives of working-class mothers and their children; at the same
time, among others, Margaret McMillan with the Independent
Labour Party agitated successfully for such reforms – school
meals, clinics and above all nurseries – as the means of raising
those same lives out of hopelessness. Two differently committed campaigners among many. A myriad examples might be
traced of other understandings of what constituted the best approach to the question of the lot of the working woman and her
children: an urgent and far-reaching question.

How were, and how are, the needs of mothers to be raised
without making a fetish out of 'motherhood', all too capable of
conservative capture? This was a difficulty for women's labour
organizations, suffrage groups, the Women's Co-Operative
Guild, women in the Labour Party and other political parties,
Fabians, feminists – a difficulty which some of them sometimes
registered or more often were not aware of. The 'sexual division
of labour' was not enunciated as a problem; improving mothers'

working lives was, especially given high rates of maternal morbidity, an obvious first task. Campaigns before and between the wars agitated for the 'endowment of motherhood' or family allowances, for access to contraception and health care, for the better state of kitchens; all these made claims to speak for the most pressing needs of women and children.

For some, it was freedom from repeated unwanted childbearing which must be won first. Dora Russell, in her *Hypatia* of 1925, held that the question of 'feminist mothers' demanded one clear response: access for all classes of women to contraception, and sexual enlightenment: 'with birth control, in two years a determined mother can completely restore her nerve, her joy in life, and her full muscular powers'. Without it, how should the working woman, badly fed and ill-housed, be expected to tolerate going on bearing children? In *Hypatia* she wrote: 'The working mother today looks straight from her kitchen, if she is lucky enough to have one, on to one of the most complex situations in history.'

Dora Russell's understanding of women's and children's needs at that point of historical complexity led her, with others, to a vision of an emancipated motherhood which combined sexual freedom with liberal child-rearing. A practical socialism, she believed, might be brought about by means of the sympathetic influence of the educated mother. She was among those whose aim, in the Worker's Birth Control Group formed in 1924, was for contraceptive information and supplies to be universally available through clinics. And Naomi Mitchison's pamphlet of 1930, *Comments on Birth Control*, also proposes the radical powers of democratic access to birth control to undercut class injustices. It, too, expresses a conviction integral to its feminism – a conviction no longer heard – that a happy heterosexuality, child-rearing and, later on, paid work, must and could combine. In this spirit, Dora Russell, in her *Defence of Children* of 1932, again inquired, 'What is a civilized mother in

the modern sense?' and provided her own answer: '. . . mothers
are seeking the liberty to do work of their own and wider choice
in loving'.

Who would take care, though, of the children did not
pose such a problem. The shadows of the housemaid and the
cook flit unmentioned behind that ordered creativity of the
emancipated socialist mother, so vigorously drawn in *Hypatia*
and in *Defence of Children*. Look also at the awkward knots of
opinion in this paragraph from the latter with its stress on
maternal maturity and its serious pleasures:

. . . female non-acceptance of maternal responsibility is deep and wide,
whether it take the form of the painted adolescence that continues to
the age of fifty years, or the grim feminist savagery that may be seen
in a body of European working-class women revolting against the
home, and demanding scientific advice that will set them free of the
burden of the hated baby. Career women, seeking not to be women at
all; alimony women, using female charm and prestige to keep afloat in
a sea of liberty and pleasure – all are in flight from the patriarchal
female pattern of dutiful daughter and self-sacrificing mother, all are
in flight from the withering and dying that inevitably follow on from
giving the body to the serious burdens of love. All, in fact, like many
men today, do not want to face the burden of growing up.

A savagery, one might think, to be espoused, and a growing up
to be fled from. The 'responsible mother' had her contradictions, which inter-war feminism was not fully able to confront.

5
Here again is Dora Russell in 1932:

There are times in history when we can no longer 'broaden down from
precedent to precedent' like the English law, and I fear that this is one
of them. Everyone feels bewildered and insecure, whether as wage-
earner or employer, wife or husband, mother or father.

Fifty years later, what can be said in the name of socialism and feminism to problems which continue to hang in another aura of 'insecurity'?

There is at the outset the question of whether a socialist feminism need object to the implied democracy of the spread of 'everyone's' insecurity. However indifferent to gender unease about the times may be, it is the case that the strain of day-to-day responsibility for the care of children does rest, on the whole, with women. Anna Martin in 1913 was decisive here:

It would be a great gain if the word 'parental' could be banished from the language for a few years. The term may refer to the father, the mother, or to both, and this ambiguity of meaning has afforded much welcome cover for obscure and confused thinking.

This is from *The Mother and Social Reform*; she had in mind the speculations of blinkered philanthropy which blamed the defects of one parent on to the other, not noticing those sharp differences in the conditions of living which were bestowed according to the sex of the parent. Her object was to pull into the light the specific position and hardships of working women as mothers; and their abilities, too. This is still an object of feminism, and it is also at odds with other objects of feminism. Child-care draws together these contesting strands – but not so as to knit them comfortingly into a smooth fabric. In brief, it is the tension between refusing to elevate maternity into some engulfing feminine principle, and demanding that the needs of mothers be met. Put so schematically, that is hardly a tension; but practically and in full detail, it is.

One solution, it has seemed to the present generation of feminists, is to argue that children are not the sole responsibility of their mothers, that their upbringing should be shared. There are many possible kinds of sharers: the state in the form of nurseries, for example, the community, friends, non-parents, fathers. I want to comment only on one of these – on 'shared parenting', since it is frequently voiced as an ideal, while its worrying properties are little mentioned. Striking among these is that it rests on the accidents of individual solutions, on individual goodwill: to make of child-care such a hostage to fortune is to depart a long way from socialist aspirations to democratically accessible community services.

The slogan of 'shared parenting' – the assertion that fathers should take equal care of their children – is a curious claimant to being a radical demand, one proper to a socialist feminism. Certainly it would entail great changes in patterns of work; it supposes some even distribution of part-time work between the sexes, and this in all kinds of employment; unless the 'sharing' were to be restricted to those who had the freedom to determine their own hours of work – or who were jobless. Here it would fit well enough, ironically, with a state of high unemployment; the Thatcher government itself has argued the virtues of work-sharing. But the arguments advanced for 'shared parenting' do not rest on its profound implications for the organization of paid work; rather that it embodies the feminist ideal that women should not be solely responsible for the care of those children which they did not, after all, produce by parthenogenesis. What a socialist feminism could have to say to the problems of child-care is hardly exhausted by the reorganization of domestic life envisaged by this particular form of care-sharing.

The redistributive justice of 'shared parenting' does not do away with the stifling couple, the dead hand of the parent: instead, all stays firmly within the family, in a way severely at odds with women's liberation aspirations about 'going outside the couple'. There is the whole question, too, of what may roughly be called power; not the 'power' of motherhood, a doubtful claim indeed, but the results of the unevenness which develops when women and men have, as is generally true, unequal access to money and work. 'Shared parenting' cannot rely on that egalitarianism which its formulation presupposes. The odds are that the sharers will start off their existence as parents on a disparate material footing; an imbalance readily exploitable in any later collapse of the goodwill which sustained the original sharing. 'Joint parenting' is also the triumph of the family-planning clinic: the rational harmonious couple, a pair of ideal social democrats who conceive their children with a truly mutual deliberation. This may be admirable, but it can – if it obscures other concerns – run too close to being a socialist social hygiene.

For where does it leave the single parent; the unhusbanded woman who prefers that state; and all those whose lives do not happen to encompass potential sharers in the upbringing of their children? How will their needs be met? Certainly there is nothing in 'shared parenting' which stands in opposition to the battles for local authority nurseries, say; the more attentions which can be alerted to the shortage of state facilities, the better. But there is the risk that concentration on the parental pair may distract from questions about what is to be done where no pair exists.

And should the sharing couple come to grief, the history of where financial power lies is likely to undermine the democracy of sharing. Once a surface of private domestic harmony is disturbed, the structures of public inegalitarianism emerge harshly. For women do not have equal chances of finding work if they have been at home with children; or of finding well-paid part-time employment. And, in the courts, a double standard of sexual morality asserts itself with a severity which mocks years of feminism; it is still, in general, true that women undergo a trial of their sexual being in a way which is not replicated for men as fathers. The sexual – at least the heterosexual – actions of a man do not throw a whole interpretative aura over his standing as a father in the eye of the law, and paternity is not thereby 'sexualized'. But maternity, though officially remote from the taint of other passions, is, with the custody of children at stake, vulnerable to judgement through the real or imputed sexual life of the mother; whether this is heterosexual, or, more dangerously, homosexual.

These lacks of symmetry between women as parents and men as parents are neither timeless, universally true nor incapable of being eroded. But while they exist they make it forcefully clear that 'parenting' cannot be confined to the private domains of the sharers, their 'personal politics' and the exercise of their wills. What can be done about the care of children is heavily invaded by the state of the labour market for both sexes, by child benefits and taxation and welfare suppositions, by the assumptions of the law courts, social workers, of all the agencies outside the home which keep a foot in the door. This is why 'shared parenting' cannot take over a great deal of rhetorical space in feminist socialist ambitions for the future of the family. As a slogan it has its uses; but they are circumscribed, and, I think, can be included with attempts at some systematic generosity, like those socialist 'good manners' which indicate that meetings ought not to be monopolized by the most obsessive speaker, that women should be equally heard, and so on. All these are excellent developments. Without them, some of us would still be stuck fast in the nervous silence in which we grew up. I, for one, am too familiar with that condition to be dismissive of any inroads on it.

These observations are *not* attacks on the principle that the existing sexual division of labour in the home and out of it should be undermined. They are cautionary remarks about letting it be implied that 'shared child-care' as a goal is capable of covering those principles adequately; that it can substitute for campaigns for nurseries, play centres, school meals, a better level of child benefit. In theory, certainly, there is no reason why these 'social' or 'community' campaigns should not exist alongside attempts to redistribute the care of children between women and men, to the greater glory of each. But what tends to happen in practice, given the utterly miserable outlook for social provisions for child-care to be extended or maintained under present conservative policy, is a loss of heart for reform in the public domain.

Instead, a fresh and anxious stress on socialist and feminist manners and conduct at home develops. This is fine; but if its limits *are* the walls of the home, then that is a constriction of feminism, which has always to look outside as well. 'Shared child-care' rests on private goodwill; but private goodwill cannot be relied on to sustain a whole politics.

The continuing battle for more, better and more flexible provision for the care of children is not, clearly, a battle to be joined only by women, by mothers. Reaffirming the old 'separate spheres' philosophy, whereby each has her or his place in the social and political order of things, will not help. Even if it is strategically necessary to agitate for child-care in terms of women's rights, to lay claim to new powers for motherhood even, what is at stake will go, in the end, beyond the sectional.

Yet it is true that feminism *is* a sectional movement; in its nature and in the point of its existence, it is 'for women'. And it is those women who are mothers who are, because of their histories, best placed now to articulate their needs; to which the needs of children can neither be simply fused, nor simply opposed. Meanwhile, the formation of a new (or the resurrection of an old) ideal of the 'socialist family' is a development we can do better without. It is *social* provision that is needed. The cry of 1940s' feminism, for paid work *and* having children, is still unanswered. For unless women chance to be protected by the fortunes of an atypically good wage, by privately afforded child-care, by a securely employed and reasonably paid husband, the truth still is that to both work and have children is, as well as a pleasure, a bitterly exhausting fight.

Sources

Aichhorn, August, *Wayward Youth*, Putnam, London, 1935.

Allen, Grant, *The Woman Who Did*, John Lane, London and Robert Bros, Boston, 1895.

Mannin, Ethel, *Common-Sense and the Child*, Jarrolds, London, 1931.

McMillan, Margaret, *Education Through the Imagination*, Swan Sonnenschein, London, 1904.

    The Child and the State, ILP, London, 1905.

    Labour and Childhood, Swan Sonnenschein, London, 1907.

    'Poverty and the Modern State' in *Present-Day Papers*, No. 3, London, 1926.

Martin, Anna, *The Married Working Woman; a Study*, NUWSS, London, 1911.

    The Mother and Social Reform, NUWSS, London, 1913.

Mitchison, Naomi, *Comments on Birth Control*, Faber and Faber, London, 1930.

Russell, Dora, *Hypatia*, Kegan Paul, Trench, Trubner & Co. Ltd, London, 1925.

    In Defence of Children, Hamish Hamilton, London, 1932.

Schmidt, Vera, and Reich, Annie, *Pulsions sexuelles et education du corps*, Union Générale d'Éditions, Paris, 1979.

Trades Union Congress General Council, *Trades Union Charter on Facilities for the Under-Fives*, TUC, London, 1978.

Trotsky, Leon, *The Revolution Betrayed*, Faber and Faber, London, 1937.

*

I am especially grateful to Deborah Thom for her comments, and for pointing me towards some of the books I have used here; to Ian Patterson for his help with references, and his comments and secretarial work; to Jonathan Rée and to Nigel Wheale for invaluable last-minute help with typing, and for suggestions. I also want to thank Carol Kendrick and Jonathan Rée for taking care of my children at times while I was writing, and Lynne Segal and Elizabeth Wilson for their editorial work.

NOTE: The address of the National Childcare Campaign is 17 Victoria Park Square, Bethnal Green, London E2.

6   Sex – A Family Affair

BEATRIX CAMPBELL

One of the shibboleths about sex is that it is a family matter. Actually, as those who face it with fear and loathing argue, it is everywhere. However, the family has historically been constructed as the site of sex and the sexualization of human beings. Sexual politics has always located analyses of sex within the family, and certainly modern feminism confronted sex within an analysis of women's subordination in the monogamous heterosexual family.

Up until the mediation of the Welfare State – which both shored up the family against its inherent instability and gave room for that instability to be resolved in different ways, not least by women getting out – women's sexuality was bound up with their economic plight as dependants.

The analysis produced by women's liberation can be summed up briefly: in Western sexual culture, male-dominated heterosexuality has conflated sex with reproduction. Reproductive sex was the model of 'normal' heterosexuality. This meant that men's orgasm, through penetration of the vagina, was the organizing principle of pleasure. It produced pregnancy, of course. And motherhood.

But one of the organizing principles of waged work, the means by which the mass of the population sustained themselves, was the exclusion of mothers from the labour market, or at best their confinement to work and wages that were barely sufficient to maintain themselves, never mind their children.

Sex meant motherhood and motherhood meant dependence. Twentieth-century sexual reform has taken these two largely as given. Its main concerns have been with protecting women from compulsive pregnancy, which was the consequence of patriarchal heterosexuality, and modifying the status of dependence within the family. This, of course, expressed the transition from sexual repression in the nineteenth century, to the establishment of heterosexuality as pleasure in the dominant ideology. Actually, to be more precise, what was at stake was the recruitment of women's participation in heterosexual pleasure within the family. But this involved a regulation of sexual practice in the twentieth century which was not so much permissive as a regulation of women as *both* sexual and subordinate.

Sexual politics has been dominated by contradictions arising within the problematic of the heterosexual family. First, the campaign for pleasure, as against purity, produced in its wake the quest for fertility control, because, of course, patriarchal heterosexuality always involved a risk – man's pleasure, woman's burden. The obstacle to women's participation was seen to be pregnancy, and thus much sexual reform was associated with the planning of pregnancy. It was not concerned with the reconstruction of sex itself. Feminist sex reformers of the 1920s were coralled into an ideological universe which took men's sexual priorities as given, and women's as the problem.

This produced a second characteristic of sexual reform within the family: the quest for female pleasure, always elusive and enigmatic, the object of agonized investigation and speculation. The working-class women who trooped through the pioneering fertility control clinics of the 1920s were not only burdened with unwanted pregnancy, but with unwanted sex, not least because, as one of the pioneering clinicians, Dr Helena Wright, observed at the time, it was assumed that women's vaginas were believed to be the answering organ to the man's penis, and were the site of their answering orgasm. This displaced the relative autonomy of the clitoris, that unique property of the female body which was about nothing if not pleasure, and nothing but pleasure. It was not that sexologists did not know about it, but that the reproductive format of sex rendered it secondary at best, or non-existent at worst.

Consequently, it was neither accidental nor euphemistic that the function of sexual reform available to working-class women was known as family planning, not pregnancy planning. Family planning was one of the most important features of modern sexual politics. Feminists active in the family planning movement have noted that the only way in which they were permitted to provide their services was to pledge that they would only be available to *married* women. It took a tough battle after the Second World War, during the so-called permissive era of the 1960s particularly, to extend pregnancy planning to women who were unmarried and whose sexual activity was, therefore, outside the pale of the family.

The early family planners often saw their concern as the reform of sexual practice within the family, and some wrote disparagingly of the single woman, who seemed to them to be somehow unfeminized by her lack of children. Many of the sexual reformers were unable to conceive of women's sexual activity outside the family and outside dependence, and thus fought for a reform of mothers' sexual opportunities and their status within dependence. So, their concern was guided to the sexual situation of mothers, rather than women in general – sexual pleasure within the familial hearth and home. This approach was undoubtedly constrained by the objective ideological conditions in which they had to operate.

However, the ideological universe into which women's liberation zoomed in the 1960s and 1970s was already rattled by instability within a family form which had nevertheless become more prevalent in British society, but which was manifestly more unstable, by the prevalence of pre-marital and extra-marital sex among women, and by the diagnosis of widespread

maternal and sexual discontentment as a kind of feminine disease. Women's liberation both felt a continuity with the early
sex reformers, and yet critical of the way in which the sexualization of women was rooted in maternity and subordination.

Two of the most important tracts which influenced women
in touch with the movement were *The Myth of Motherhood* by
Lee Comer[1] and *The Myth of the Vaginal Orgasm* by Anna
Koedt.[2] The structure of the movement – small groups committed to speaking out feelings which had been experienced
hitherto as pathological and which were now political – enabled
the family to be produced as a political problematic. Everything
in it was questioned, from nappies to orgasms, monogamy and
money.

Sexual politics have been identified with women's liberation,
and yet are also the issue upon which feminists have felt most
divided, leaving them feeling gobsmacked internally and often
bewildered about the relevance of sexuality strategically to
women *en masse*, or particularly that most coveted and elusive
subject of socialist struggle, the working-class woman. It is
important to recall, however, the lasting innovations of feminist
campaigns around sexual politics within the family. This is
important not only to establish that women's liberation has had
effect, but to serve as a reminder that any evacuation from
personal politics in relation to the heterosexual family is to
evacuate from the project of women's liberation itself.

The most obvious example perhaps is the seemingly infinite
energy which feminism has had to devote to the defence of
abortion and contraception rights established in the 1960s, in
the face of direct assaults on the law itself by Conservative and
Labour MPs, and from the strangling of National Health Service facilities available to women. There have been several other
campaigns which have confronted the effect upon women of
the heterosexual family, ranging across schooling, the construction of femininity, sexism in advertising, police practices in

relation to rape and assault, sexual abuse of girls and women's financial dependence. The fact is that women's liberation has raised the sexual oppression of women on to the national political stage, and has transcended the boundaries of the movement's early sexual politics.

What this has involved is campaigns to change the consciousness of men and women in the situations in which men's sexual dominance is secured. For example, Women's Aid is perhaps a paradigm of this refinement of feminist politics and brings feminists into a direct confrontation with the forces concerned with consolidating the family. In establishing refuges in many cities up and down the country, it has challenged the institutional and financial constraints operating through housing policy, employment, supplementary benefits, the role of police and social services, and finally the law, which forced women to stay in marriages which put their person at risk.

The refuges provided concrete facilities outside the state system, and combined the provision of sanctuary with a political approach which was not dogmatic and did not impose yet more injunctions on the women themselves either to leave home or to return. In that sense, it provided a space for women, perhaps for the first time in their lives, to have a taste of the limits and possibilities of self-determination.

It is a commonplace complaint that women's liberation alienates the mass of women and stands apart from them. But the network of refuges provides 'ordinary' women, 25,000 of them every year, with safe passage for themselves and their children, as well as a resource which will help them to negotiate with the labyrinth of state agencies whose object is to do the opposite. Feminism was also confronted by forms of political negotiation from which it had been excluded, with the state for funding, physical space and resources, while retaining control over the administration of refuges.

In doing so it has provided a safety from the extremities of male dominance in the heterosexual family. More than that, it has provided a resourced response to crisis within the family which enables women to see it, rather than simply themselves, as the problem. For the Women's Aid movement has insisted that it is the family itself, and not just unaccountably crazy men, that produces violence against women, and that, like rape, it is sexually specific. It is about men's power as men.

Refuges came out of the experience rather than the theory of feminism. But this is not to suggest that theory has not been part of the movement's arsenal to defend itself against critics in social services and psychology, and even the Women's Aid pioneer, Erin Pizzey. They have tried to weaken feminism's critique of the dynamic of dominance and subordination in the family by the old myth that battering can be explained as the pathological sadism of individual men and the masochism of individual women, thus exempting the institution and culture of the family from critical analysis.

If the 1970s brought out woman-torture, the 1980s has brought children's sexual oppression in the family out of the closet and faced a culture obsessed with the protection of children from sex with an epidemic of sexual oppression of children, particularly of girls by their fathers.

Incest is quintessentially a family matter, and a classic example of the need to review our theories of repression. For incest is a sin, a crime, and it is the family's great skeleton in the cupboard. The Incest Survivors Group has politicized the issue by bringing women together, out of the isolated confidentiality of the confessional, and by its assault on the fortifications of grief, guilt, shame and blame by the very use of its self-description: survivors.

Rape Crisis Centres have likewise provided women with the means of clawing their way out of shame and self-hatred, and have challenged popular wisdom about how and when rape actually happens. This paralleled the national preoccupations with the cases of the Cambridge rapist in the 1970s and the Yorkshire Ripper, which were characterized by staggering police bungling and virtual curfews on women. The anti-rape movement exposed the fallacies created by media fetishes with cases like these, by showing that most rapes involve men known to the women, often members of their family. Patriarchal revenge meted out against other men's sexual crimes against women incited 'hang 'em and flog 'em' expletives among the seemingly mildest of men, while it apparently does not occur to them that it is something that only men do.

What neither their avenging spleens, nor some feminist campaigns against pornography seem to assimilate, is that the main site of sexual abuse of women and children is *in* the family. This, therefore, demands political strategies about the family. But although our concern is with sexual politics and the family, it is important to register other campaigns which fall outside this parameter: pornography and sexual harassment.

Sexual objectification has always been a target of women's liberation, from the flour-bombing of the 'Miss World' contest in 1970, to campaigns against sexist advertising, which has more recently been elaborated into a rich seam of guerrilla graffiti. The recent wave of sexual terror movies provoked a wave of direct action at cinemas by women's groups in many cities, and women have marched through areas like Soho to 'reclaim the night'. Concern with sexual violence and pornography coalesced in the Women Against Violence Against Women, a movement which seized many women's political imagination.

It is also one which has prompted feminist criticism, both because of the risk of representing women as powerless victims, producing political gestures as against consequential strategies which actually change people, basing a politics on an axis of weakness and terror, and tending to conflate all erotic representations of women as incitement to oppress women.

Sexual harassment at work has become the target of

trade-union action, initiated by the public sector union
NALGO, and since adopted by several other unions. This
registers work as a sphere of sexual interaction, and also expands
the boundaries of sexual politics into collective bargaining. It
does this in a remarkable way, for it forces trade unions to
recognize a conflict of interest between male and female members. It also has the potential of *specifying* sexism by identifying
legitimate complaints against jokes, calendars, atmosphere,
touching and assault – in other words, all the normal
paraphernalia of workplaces.

Lesbianism has already been mentioned as an expression of
female sexuality outside the family, although it must be said
that lesbians are not necessarily outside the family, something
which heterosexual people, not least feminists, rather readily
forget. Lesbians are in many respects just like other women,
something which is, perhaps, too subversive a notion to bear.

There is a dread of the lesbian mother, typified by the state
of the courts. Lesbians fighting for custody of their children
lose. They're caught in a 'catch-22' – to win custody means
denying their lesbianism. And it is not simply a one-off re-
pudiation for the courtroom: custody is always open to review,
and fathers can return to the courts with evidence about the
mothers' friends and lovers. Lesbians' lawyers tend to advise
them that, if they fight as lesbians, they will lose. A widely
reported case in Scotland involved a mother of a teenager. She
won custody on condition that the child was brought up heterosexual. Despite gay liberation and all that positive thinking,
how many progressive parents would come out and say that
they are *happy* for their daughters to be lesbians.

The relationship between lesbianism and heterosexuality is
critical for the modern women's movement, which, like its
predecessors, may feel moved to shrink from the alliance. The
retreat is grounded in the notion that the sexuality of lesbians
and heterosexual women is essentially different – when what

may be really at stake is that heterosexuality is rooted in a familial sexual ideology, from which it has never managed to shake itself free. By this is meant the construction in ideology of heterosexual sex.

First, women have been heterosexualized in an unprecedented way in the space of a couple of generations. Celibacy and spinsterhood have stopped being the reality they once were in women's lives, if we are to take seriously the trends in marriage over the century. The proportion of women who marry has steadily increased throughout this century.[3] Women have become encircled by men. The heterosexual, monogamous marriage was *the* sexual and domestic norm in a way that it had not been. Some may have viewed this as progressive evolution, but it can also be seen as an intense regulation of women's sexuality. Any other than married heterosexuality and motherhood was marginalized, and certainly deviant. Coincident with the mobilization of marriage was a massive ideological manoeuvre against the sexual autonomy of women – the construction of the concept of the sexual act itself.

This assertion should not be confused with that propounded by some feminists that the actual penetration of the vagina by the penis constitutes the invasion of a woman's person, and that capitulation to it involves at best deviancy and at worst collaboration with the enemy. Rather it is to argue that the reduction of sexual acts to the sexual act is a historical process, that it involves the subordination or suppression of women's own sexual interests to the moment of penetration, which is represented as the sexual moment.

The effect of this concept is to represent lesbianism as incomplete, and heterosexual women dependent on the penis as the organizing principle of sex. It achieves this by describing the model sexual act as an orgasmic symmetry engineered by penetration.

Anna Koedt's *Myth of the Vaginal Orgasm* asserted that men

were doggedly resistant to the claims of the clitoris, and she identified penetration as a major fortification in patriarchal sexuality. One effect of this work was to generate a sense of women's body which could ally heterosexual, homosexual and celibate women. As we have said earlier, lesbians' pleasure was in femaleness, rather than a refusal of the female – something which heterosexuality has still not registered.

What ought perhaps to have been acknowledged rather more was that not only did lesbianism have no problem about the clitoris, but neither did it have any problem about the vagina, which for many lesbians is simply another place of pleasure. But then pleasure and sexual politics cannot, of course, be reduced to the anatomy. Much feminist work is being done on representations of women in ideology and analysis of the construction of the feminine subject. Much more needs to be understood about the meaning attached to the body, rather than assuming that the body somehow speaks for itself.

Yet there is still more at stake, which is to do with our construction as heterosexual or homosexual persons. These are categories which the women's liberation movement has uniquely subverted. Within the movement's ambit, many women underwent a sexual metamorphosis as the taboo on lesbianism was lifted. Some women with a primarily heterosexual practice have acknowledged that they do not feel themselves to be heterosexual people so much as people whose activity is sometimes heterosexual.

There are also some feminists (not to mention women at large, of course) who insist upon a heterosexual identity which refuses any identification with homosexuality, save at the level of supporting its civil rights. They repudiate lesbianism on the grounds that it has got nothing to do with them, or lament that it is just another index of women's liberation's distance from ordinary women.

The effect is to short-circuit a debate about sexuality which would be revolutionary. These are some of the issues which must inform a theoretical perspective adequate to challenge men's control of women's sexuality through the regulation of the monogamous, heterosexual family.

Notes and References

1. Lee Comer, *The Myth of Motherhood*, Partisan Press, Nottingham, 1971.
2. Anna Koedt, *The Myth of the Vaginal Orgasm*, in L. Tanner (ed.), *Voices from Women's Liberation*, New American Library, New York, 1971.
3. Jeffrey Weeks, *Sex, Politics and Society. The Regulation of Sexuality since 1800*, Longman, London, 1981.

Home Thoughts from Not So Far Away: A Personal Look at Family

WENDY CLARK

The Royal Wedding was roundly berated in feminist and socialist circles. The feminist critique has tended to focus on marriage and the dependency of a married woman on a man. Socialists have raised the same issue and also added capitalist exploitation of the workers who produced royal paraphernalia, the institution of royalty and the way housing, unemployment, racism and political oppression were pushed off the front pages. The righteous indignation at the event and its subsequent sequel produced badges and slogans galore. No self-respecting feminist would have been without her 'Don't Do It, Di!' badge; though my personal favourite was the one that said, 'You have to kiss an awful lot of frogs to find a prince!' The new popular equivalent is, 'Save the Royal Baby, Join CND!' As I began writing this, the papers were full of special anniversary photos of Charles and Diana and baby William. The family is in the news again, properly sanctified and blessed by the nation. Feminist friends said some commendably derogatory things when viewing the pictures, but as I listened and joined in I became aware that we all had rather sickly soporific smiles on our faces, *of which we were wholly unaware*. We were saying one thing but our expressions were giving other messages – living our contradictions on the subject of the family.

Contradictions: Christmas pudding or muesli pie?

Apart from men, one thing which feminists love to hate is the family. Condemnation of the family and what it stands for has been one of the mainstays of feminist theory and practice. Hostility to the family was not new to feminism, it had been around socialist circles for some years. However, what feminism did was to take its hostility seriously and incorporate its critique in its theory and practice.

Yet, in spite of the heavy critiques, I never fail to be astonished at the annual migration of feminists, socialists and other anti-family persons back to the bosom of the family at Christmas time. There are few that can ignore the pull of such an occasion. Those who do ignore the pull find it incredibly difficult to organize an alternative feminist, or even socialist, Christmas. As the time gets closer, more and more friends, in somewhat mixed emotional states, set off home for the mandatory five days. Many return swearing, 'Never again!' but the annual pilgrimages continue. Our rhetoric leaves a hefty gap in explanations which can cover such strange and basically 'incorrect' behaviour. Christmas, of all times in the year, is *the* time when we can see and experience the awfulness of families: mother slaving over the food, father carving the turkey, children opening the presents; all pretending it's great; spending far more than they can afford, watching family entertainment on TV, getting on each other's nerves but smiling in spite of it; mother and daughter washing the dishes, father and son shovelling the snow from the door, perhaps a foray to church. Why would any self-respecting feminist want to return to such a patriarchal, oppressively demeaning, stereotypic social setting? Even if only once a year? It can't be just to reassure ourselves of the horribleness of families; memories are more than enough for that purpose!

In all that has been written by feminists and socialists about the family, it is such immediate contradictions that are seldom addressed. Yet, regardless of all rhetoric and theory, the family does have an ideological hold on us all. For feminists in particular who live outside the traditional family and attempt to

create new forms of living, there are real problems which still
remain unanswered.

Unhappy Families: or what to think about when you can't get the card you want

The family has become a catchall phrase for everything that
we, as feminists, condemn in our society. Family equals oppression, patriarchy, psychosis, neurosis, domestic labour, role
stereotyping, gender specific definitions, stifling relationships,
fathers, mothers, sisters, brothers, children, financial dependence, marriage, sexual repression, sexual activity, heterosexuality, growing up, living, dying, tradition, delinquency, love,
hate, incest, violence, battering and bad eating habits. It is a
source of many of the oppressive mechanisms which feminists
continue to work towards changing or replacing. It can therefore still feel very much like defeat to be drawn into experiences which are so heavily linked to the family, such as
monogamous relations, jealousy, stereotyping or going home
for Christmas.

Betty Friedan says in *The Second Wave*: 'I believe that feminism must in fact confront the family, albeit in new terms, if
the movement is to fulfil its revolutionary function in modern
society . . .' Few feminists would disagree with the need to
confront the family, but we are as divided as our socialist
brothers on how to do it and on what terms the debate should
be held. Other sections of this book cover its history, the feminist critiques, the role of children, state policies and women's
dependence. Yet whatever we say about these areas, we are left
with the living reality of our own lives. It is against this that we
measure our conceptions of this most invidious and yet so
apparently essential of institutions. Yet there are questions
which I find hard to answer. I wonder what our experiences of
the last eleven years show and whether there are aspects of the

family which merit some re-examination? This chapter contains thoughts and some indications of what some of these may be.

Defining: or 'Now everyone wants to play'

The family attempts to meet some extremely diverse social and personal needs. Many of us have been trying to create alternatives that meet these needs without those aspects which oppress us and our children. The traditional nuclear form of the family is changing with more one-parent families, an increase in working mothers, divorce and remarriage. Interest in the ideal family and the processes associated with the family forms continues, however, unabated in spite of such changes. If the form is changing, just alter the definition. From the White House Conference on Families comes:

Two or more persons who share resources, share responsibility for decisions, share values and goals, and have commitments to one another over time. The family is that climate that one 'comes home to', and it is this network of sharing and commitments that most accurately describes the family unit, regardless of blood, legal ties, adoption or marriage.

Many different persons and groupings of people are re-examining the family, and it sometimes seems that pressure groups join with women on the fringes of feminism to push us back into the old form rather than forward to a new radicalism.

A spate of books and articles on the family and aspects of it has been appearing recently. They range from Betty Friedan's *Second Wave* to Ferdinand Mount's *The Subversive Family*. *New Socialist* and *Marxism Today* have both carried prominent articles on aspects of the family. *Cosmopolitan* and *Honey* and *19* have all shown considerable interest in violence and sexual abuse in families. And from across the Atlantic, reverberations of the heavy debate around a pro-family left group called 'Friends of Families' come to us via *Socialist Review*.

But how far are feminists keeping up with these re-examinations of one of our most basic building blocks? Has our focus on the negative, oppressive and neurotic aspects of families meant that our analysis of what they may provide beyond that suffered? Even if we hate our families, we carry them around with us for ever and define our alternative life-styles always in oppositional terms. For our generation, and even the one after us, a family of sorts was there at our beginnings and will be there to the end in us, whether we like it or not. A reluctance to dissect the family and its functions properly forces it to become like the state, men and capitalism – a vague monolithic conception that has to be fought at every turn. There are aspects of the function and form of the family which all feminists would want to change, but it does not necessarily follow that there is nothing worth keeping. It is, indeed, unfortunate that much of the rethinking of this question is coming from women representing the 'liberal right' of the feminist movement.

State of Play: 'The rules of the game are not what they seem'

The women's movement has fought hard for change that would give us all more choice and control over our lives. To this end, the oppressive family scenario has been one of the mainstays of feminist analysis. The women's movement has tried to break down gender roles and divisions in families and divisions between home and work. It has countered views that women's exclusive role is mothering and nurturing; that the seat of authority in the home is the father; that working mothers neglect their children; that women can't have a career and a child; that men expect women to service them in the home; that children have to be raised as role-gendered boys and girls and that men wouldn't enjoy being present at the birth of children. Our politics and social theories have said much about these aspects of family and their intrinsically oppressive power over women and children. Many of these things have been countered, and the opposite of them is now far more commonly found in many kinds of family unit. Of course, not everyone has all of them, but they are a possibility, more so than ten years ago. After many weary years of struggle with male colleagues and partners, there are areas of hard-won equality that can be maintained, albeit after endless negotiation and discussion. But the wearying day-to-day struggle to maintain men's commitment to non-gendered activities is seldom on any analytical agenda. What feminists also know is that sexual matters, power, jealousy, commitment, fatherhood, security, autonomy and growth are seldom as open to negotiation and analysis. Are these such overwhelming problems for us that it seems a defeat even to be drawn into discussing this aspect of family?

It is within these parameters that the real struggle over the family has to take place. Feminism (with the aid of some socialists) has concentrated on the far more visibly oppressive nature of the family. Perhaps that was the way to start and gains have been made. But we are left with the far less tangible aspects of the family, the unspoken and the hidden. The new definitions of family and an increasing use of the term 'family units' are wide enough to take many of our new households and alternative styles into account and even encourage them if need be. In the rest of this chapter I will raise some of the elements which I think are here for examination. I feel they spring from fundamental and deeply rooted aspects of family, and for the long-term future of feminism they need to be tackled and if possible answered.

Home or Family: or 'Mixed communal house reqs Soc-'em to share, o/r, cat, CH, non-smoking (if possible)'

Changing the way women, children and men relate to each

other has been given a political as well as personal significance by the feminist movement. All of us have particular needs that appear possible to meet only in family or close dependency substitute households. Many feminists have spent much of the last ten years or more establishing, maintaining and analysing these substitute households. How far are they alternatives to family and how far do they meet our stringent requirements? If we alter the patriarchal position of men and all the family forms that come from that and eliminate the dependency of women on men's financial offerings, what do we have left? The debris of innumerable communal households litters our social arenas. Out of the debris we grow and change, but the cost is heavy. It seems to me that we have become very good at establishing and maintaining households of all kinds where the form of the family model has been drastically altered. Tasks are shared, rotas adhered to, child-care arrangements managed – tolerable, relatively relaxed households where all the gendered roles and patriarchal expectations have been banished to the back shed. In appearance, it all looks very good. But our house-holds still come and go, disintegrate and reform. We know the 'normal' family also breaks up at a phenomenal rate. But it is not good enough to accept the inevitability of break-up. We no longer have the excuse of 'oppressive family' so that the con-tinual disintegration and reforming of collective households should be a matter for serious questioning. There are a whole number of conditions and aspects of living with others which continue to interrupt our pursuit of our ideal. The boundaries of the hidden, discreet areas of living with others are where our endeavours so often come unstuck. Dealing with emotionality, our needs to be needed, our desires for autonomy and independence, friendship, companionship, dependency, com-mitment, vulnerability, closeness, caring, worrying, personal space, demands, isolation, fears, stress and sex. It is around these areas that the dynamics of our new alternatives founder.

Combining household with support and security has always been a problematic resolution for those of us trying to live outside anything which is of the traditional form. Our new household forms are based not on kinship and dependency, but instead on sexual relationships (heterosexual, homosexual or lesbian), or friendship networks, interest groups, or none of these but merely through ads in the alternative press. The companionship and support which should be the family's traditional offer is either grafted on to the alternative household or acquired elsewhere by the communards. The former solution has not been easy. It has often not proved entirely possible to artificially create the closeness and warmth and acceptance which often comes from family life and certainly comes from our ideal conception of 'home'. The family/home dichotomy is important and it can and does place certain demands on to our living situations which can be difficult for the new situation to meet as rapidly as we may wish it to do. Do alternative households ever resolve this dichotomy? Can they re-create 'home' and leave behind 'family'?

Collective or Communal: does it matter?

Over the years, together with other feminists and socialists, we have been part and parcel of this search for a viable alternative. Hand in hand with this went our implicit and often open challenge of the assumptions of our 'old' family groups. More recently, there have been changes in our living arrangements and some reorientation of our expectations. Many women are facing the decisions over children, to have or not, by ourselves or with another; others are involved in buying homes and agonizing over Highgate or Clapham; others are facing critical crisis points in relationships; many of us are questioning our political activities and orientations, socialist-feminist or feminist and socialist? And sex and sexuality is becoming a key question in our lives again.

Alternative households, which attempted to be big collective living spaces, are turning into pseudo-family groups based around several monogamous relationships; the well-balanced house these days would have a mixture of heterosexual and gay (men or women) couples, possibly two single (but settled) persons and one or two children (with possibilities of others), and of course a cat or two. All of these alternative households, unlike families, are a loose association of persons of the same age group artificially brought together by economic necessity and ideological theory. They are initially bound by little else. The ties between this diverse group of people have to be painfully constructed. It has never been easy, and whenever a crisis has struck the household and people move out or in, the whole process has begun all over again. One household that I lived in for four years saw eleven individual personnel changes, and that did not count the various relationships which came and went and countless visitors in the 'spare room'. Wedded as we all were to a new collective ideal, the drain on our resources and emotions was debilitating. Many of the eleven now live alone, though some of us are moving back into living with others, but with vastly changed perspectives and a far more realistic attitude.

A multitude of scattered remnants of innumerable collective households litter our social networks. Yet we must remember that we worked hard at creating a strong family substitute arrangement. One collective household devoted one wall of a living room to a collage of photos of 'ancestors' and themselves at various stages of growth and development. It was almost as if, since the generation and age-range basis of the family could not be created in reality, they were doing so by proxy. Visitors often felt extremely uncomfortable in this house and reported that visiting was rather like being introduced to parents in early courtship stages. The re-creation was completed in the morning as the household always had breakfast together, so that if anyone had a stranger to stay over-night, household members *and* ancestors had to be faced. This seldom occurred. After all, parents at breakfast are one of the things we've been trying to escape. However, in spite of their attempt to create a closeness and a history for their household, this one went the way of so many others. Happily the feminists involved still have a very strong set of relationships with each other which are described as like sisters with much of the unconditional acceptance which is connected with our ideal view of close family ties.

Throughout what I have been saying in this section, I am becoming aware that one of the problems that we have not really been able properly to come to grips with lies in the difference between 'collective' and 'communal' households. We tend to use the two terms interchangeably when in fact I think they indicate and distinguish between two quite different forms of household. When I look back on living situations that I've been involved in or had contact with, we really have got things messed up. On the one hand, we have created 'collective' households which seem to be based on stating what you need and want, what you will or won't do, and negotiating around these areas. I hate rotas, and lists and tasks, and it's my turn to and your turn to, and why haven't you done?! It's never: 'It's nice to see what you did in . . .' And it has taken me until now really to figure out what is going on. My ideal is what I would distinguish as 'communal' rather than 'collective'.

Here limits and responsibilities come together and are integral to the total set-up. Everyone's contribution is recognized and there will be no need for a rota. We will all just get on with it; if it is to be done it will be done, and what you may see as your responsibility today may be different tomorrow. It is a sad commentary on our socialization and old family forms that we need all that *organizing* to be collective, and that unless it's written down it won't be done. The last person to use a toilet roll is the one to replace it, not the one whose job it is to look after the bathroom. We all use the bathroom so we all have responsibility! My ideal has room for autonomy and responsibility, shared and not proscribed, no need for rotas, and organizing is kept to the minimum. The problem is, though, that the ideal is not the way it always works. Some 'brothers' and 'sisters' just do not seem to have much collective responsibility, let alone common sense, so in the end we often still need the rotas or else it is just one or two who end up doing it all. But I would *like* us to move on from all that and get down to the *real* business of living with others.

Bad Experiences: or 'Preoccupied with sex or rather the lack of it'

Sex is everywhere; not always where we'd like it to be, but it lurks about in likely places. One of these which it favours is among those of us struggling to create feminist alternatives to the family. And when sex enters the household, whatever its alternative form, it intrinsically alters the balance and the household dynamics. We often try to assert that it shouldn't have this effect, but in most instances I can recall or have had recounted to me, it does change things and therefore cannot be ignored.

Alternative living groupings have either been predicated on no sexual ties between members or are created around couples with a sexual relationship. Where sexual relationships are present, there often tend to be created mini-systems within the household. Households which have no sexual ties can often create a closeness which, for a time, can be similar to better aspects of family solidarity, *or* they can be very separate in their relationships with each other. Whatever the composition of the household, the dynamic will be slightly different in each case.

But the sexual dynamic will be ever present whatever the composition. In addition, the sexual orientation of the household members – lesbian, homosexual, heterosexual or bi-sexual – will also have its effect on the sexual dynamic.

Even the traditional family is created out of sex and the sexual dynamics of these families have been well charted by psychoanalysis and feminist theorists. All families, outside of our alternative collectives, whether nuclear, extended, separated or one-parent, are the result of a heterosexual sexual relationship (albeit a short-lived one). As we know to our cost, the sexual side of these households is hidden and often unacknowledged. The incest taboo controls the sexual element in most forms of families and circumscribes the limits of relationships. Consequently, the accepted family forms have two edges to most things: the good tinged with the bad, or the bad tinged with the good, however you wish to view it. In a sense it is a hot-bed of sexual desires and emotions, unspoken and hidden but present and supremely important for our personal and sexual growth and identity: self-construction through a fundamental and oppressive lie.

It is in the area of personal oppression and sexuality that we often find a need for individual confrontation of inherent assumptions in our personal family groups. Perhaps the most confronting practice available to us is possible only for some. I refer to the process of 'coming out' as lesbian or gay to your family. The emphasis on coming out has been a vital tactic which translates the personal into the political. It is possibly the ultimate challenge to the old family forms, challenging, as it does, the heterosexual assumptions and the hidden psychosexual processes of all families. Significant though it might be, it is, however, very, very difficult to do. There are many women and men I know who are quite open and 'out' in their work and social life but still have not told their parents. We criticize, alter, confront and re-create on almost every other visible aspect of the family we dislike, but we still find it so hard to share the very personal. The reasons women and men have for not telling are many, but in the end I think some of the essence of why not is contained in, 'I don't know what I'd do if they "reacted". I don't know if I could cope.' There are few lesbians or gay men who would take satisfaction from being rejected by their family. We feel that we probably will be if we do tell, but the imperative to share is there. What I find interesting is that in so many cases I know of, the family has not rejected. The initial response *is* often shock and disbelief, but seldom the, 'Don't darken my doorstep again.' Horror stories do occur, and I would not want to underrate them. But what I find interesting, in the context of this chapter, is that the need to belong and be accepted and the fear of rejection is stronger than anything 'the neighbours might think'.

I recall being obsessed with telling my parents but never really being able to for a long time. Other family members knew, but they did not (or so I thought). In spite of all the trappings of an alternative life-style, I needed them to know. Why I took so long was primarily to do with rejection. I might criticize many things, but to be cast aside by parents would be terrifying and I seriously thought it would happen. However, the internal desire was stronger and the deed was done and I was not rejected. The relief was tremendous. Acceptance and recognition from friends and work-mates was nothing in the face of the sense of freedom and exhilaration I had from family recognition. The contradictions around support and security needs and the oppression of the sexual lies of the family make coming out particularly difficult. I wonder if any heterosexual, no matter how much they confront their families, ever has to face such a crucial decision as that one facing lesbians and gay men. The sexual norms of the family and its unspoken role are confronted head-on in coming out. Nothing else can have such an effect on the family.

Playing the Game: 'Now you see it, now you don't'

Alternative households usually have considerable problems with hidden sexuality. It is not possible to banish sex out of their domestic lives. It may not even be right to do so. On the one hand, we recognize the oppression of sex in our families and do not want to live that way any more. On the other hand, it has to be dealt with as it is often various forms of incestuous activities and desires which cause crisis and break-up. In the collective situation I have already described (page 176), the hidden desires exploded to the surface, which they are not supposed to do in well-regulated, normal living. Trying to be unlike the family but like the ideal, sex was hidden and was never discussed inside the house, even as a subject for house meetings. This generally continues to be so. But adults are used to pursuing their needs. The hidden bursts into the open and all hell breaks loose.

If we accept that the way the family is constructed answers certain of our desires and sexual needs and contributes to personal growth through this, it could then follow when we attempt to copy aspects of what went before, these needs and desires are still around; albeit unconsciously hidden. Mostly families contain them and keep them hidden, but our adult alternatives are established on a strongly reactive basis. Therefore they often have considerable problems dealing with the sexual when it occurs in the household. One way we deal with it is to banish it from the household or confine it only to 'couples' in the house. The support you get from others is therefore dependent on, 'No sex with each other and for God's sake don't talk about it either!' Some cope by ignoring it for as long as possible, which ultimately creates such tensions that the bricks come tumbling down. Why is it so hard for our brave new worlds to contain this? Are our emotional ties with each other not strong enough? Can we allow it to become so obvious that it is never hidden? Or do we thrill to the opportunity to eventually let out all that we had to repress in our old family?

There is something in the way that ideological and psychological structures work in families that generally contains all this and turns it into part of our psycho-sexual development. As adults, we have presumably passed that phase and a large part of our selves and our sexual identities cannot be accommodated in the same way. No longer hidden, we know we can have.

There is much in this context that we do not know and which our experimental households have been unable to resolve. Another collective household, together for even more years than the one already mentioned, crashed when one of the women asked if one of the men could co-parent a child with her. The house refused to allow it. They had not been averse to sex partners through ads in *Time Out* as long as they remained outside the house and did not involve reproduction. The request to transgress the sexual taboos was met with stoney refusal and an insensitive lack of understanding. The structures of support and emotionality they had so carefully built up could not cope with this major request. The woman and one of the men left and the household slowly disintegrated. Yet another alternative to the family had foundered through an inability to cope with an aspect of sex. In a sense, it was like the family we all seek to escape from so determinedly. If we keep it hidden and remote, we can cope, but if it comes out into the open, we can't. Yet if it is alternatives that we are about, then why can't we cope? Not that it is any easier with outside sex partners either. Our familial siblings' sex partners we may not like, but we learn to accept and live with; we have to if we want to keep our ties with them. If we live collectively with other feminists and/or men, we can be damningly critical of their sex partners. After all, we don't have to adjust to them like we do to family. For the couples involved, often the only refuge is for them to leave or lock themselves away from the others.

We are conscious of the way sexual involvement does change relationships at basic and fundamental levels, but we have not devised a method to deal with it very well. Sometimes we act no better than the family we try to avoid. Are we playing out childhood games unresolved with our parents, with our friends? Are we afraid that when friends become sexually involved with others, they will desert us, not like us any more? Instead of trying to banish the sexual from our living circumstances and support and friendship networks, we should work out how to talk about it and perhaps cope with it.

Afterwards: or 'Orgasm isn't enough'

In spite of the problems, all is not gloom. There are aspects to the sex and support system which some feminists are grappling with relatively successfully, and in so doing are showing others new possibilities. Too frequently, when sex relations have ended, that has been the end of support and commitment. Bitterness, denial, anger, hatred and indifference can follow, and mostly do. Many feminists have considered this a time-consuming and retrograde aspect of personal relationships. There are signs that there are support networks crossing households based on relationships that were sexual and are no longer so. Former lovers remain especially strong and committed friends, particularly if the relationship was of a lengthy duration. I am unsure, though, how far this is something largely confined to lesbian feminists? The experiences of heterosexual couples is different, and I cannot speak with authority about them.

From observation, the bitterness which often accompanies break-ups is more pronounced among heterosexual couples. The dynamics of their relationships are different from lesbians' or gay men's, and even if they are trying to redefine and recreate new forms, patriarchy, power and heterosexism continue to make moving on painful and extremely difficult. But it would be comforting to those of us trying to come to terms with these problems if it could be that the end of a sexual relationship did not mean the end of that relationship. Is it possible that having faced and then removed sex could mean that our expectations in the relationship alter considerably and we give up expecting everything from our lovers as we have had to give up expecting everything from the family? Relationships that survive beyond sex are frequently left with a strong commitment and acceptance of each other similar to aspects of the support we would wish to have from family links. It is not an easy area for any of us, and sometimes it is not possible to get past the trauma, but it is encouraging that more women (and men?) are trying to do so. Some feminists would say that all this is no different from the way women support each other anyhow – that sex has little to do with it. I cannot agree, as it does seem to me that having had a strong sexual relationship and all that entails with another woman (or man) does mean that, if you continue a relationship with your ex-lover, it *must* be different from other relationships. The shared experience of a long sexual relationship is not entirely the same as 'woman-to-woman' relationships. It is based on a 'knowing' that goes beyond friendships and in the end comes closer to the familial sister or brother.

Ideals and Realities: or 'I think I'll collect the Buns!'

Another area of family concern that comes into play when we try to play 'substitute families' is raised by the question, 'What does the family mean to you?' When I asked some feminists this question, I was struck by the almost universal response, which can best be described, as one woman put it, as 'unconditional belonging that doesn't necessarily entail affection'. It is a hope for the experience of the ideal and not necessarily what we know our families exhibit. We would like to experience in all our living circumstances the ideal of intangible and variable sentiments which revolve around personal loyalties, warmth, closeness, familiarity and being part of something which will accept you, warts and all. Neither our families nor our new living arrangements necessarily provide this ideal. Sometimes families do accept, at other times they do not. Our memories of acceptance will be mixed and invariably will affect the expectations we have of our living situations.

I have a very pronounced limp. Yet, as a small child, for some time I was not aware of it, nor were my brother, sister or numerous cousins. We'd all express surprise when outsiders commented on it. It was simply not noticed since it was 'just the way I was'. In contrast to that acceptance, when I came out to the family certain members gave a much more guarded acceptance, such as, 'Don't tell your brother, it will only upset him.' Some warts will be handled, others are more problematic. I am sure that readers will have had similar experiences.

We enter the family as children and we leave it as adults, and it is what happens, or what we *think* should have happened, that we are always trying to re-create or recast. It is not just alternative domestic arrangements, new child-care forms or sharing household tasks – we are also constantly searching for the less tangible aspects of what it all means to us. And we constantly become confused by the reality and the ideal. Whenever I feel depressed, I think of home and family; whenever another woman thinks of home and family, she becomes depressed. It is contradictions like this that prevent the alternative households we create from working for as long and as effectively as we would like.

They should work! They are founded on a rational re-allocation of resources and tasks and a firm theoretical basis from our feminist theory. However, it is because they are not working properly and are often a poor imitation of our ideal that feminism needs to look more closely at them. We must ask what needs they are not meeting, and whether our flight from the family is just surface deep, and whether the underlying form that we have created is any different in substance from what we so fiercely criticize.

The Game Continues: or 'Why the rules do not explain everything'

I try not to idealize the family. I live outside it and, as a lesbian, will never be able to join it properly. But I will also not idealize our attempts at new collective living arrangements. Difference does not equal better all the time. I feel that there is something missing from our theory which can help us to explain and cope with the constant battle we all have against reality and ideals. There are too many feminists, myself included, doing many of the things of which we would be extremely critical if they occurred in a nuclear family setting. I do not think that the missing parts need to be darkly obscure psychoanalytic explanations inaccessible to all but the converted. However, they must offer more hope in helping us to reconcile some of the contradictions which we live every day. None of us wish to re-create our 'sad, sadistic families'; but our ideals are also hard to live up to.

Outside feelings and needs have to be negotiated and are dependent on other adults who want exactly the same as you. One thing the family allowed us as children was to demand and demand; whether we ever got it was another matter. Yet we must not forget that the family was also a place of danger and that we could be overwhelmed by it. Are we taking the danger out of our new situations? Our struggle to keep and establish autonomy comes out of possible and real rejection, as well as the fear of being merged in an all-embracing suffocation.

Families attempt a balance between social needs and the individuals' desires. In our choices we may opt for the social at the expense of desire, and sometimes at the cost of our new experiments. Probably unconsciously, we do end up opting for something that is similar to that from which we flee, or an extremely precarious balance. Outside of the family we can choose. We can choose our friends, our lovers and our life-styles. And we can choose these again, and again, and again. Our parents, sisters and brothers we cannot change. They are stuck with us and we with them. Even if you are like me and see little of them, they exist in me and with me because they are so much a part of my development. Friends, lovers and households can and do come and go, and sometimes they do *ad infinitum*. Seldom do they elicit the same and instantaneous responses as family does.

Why should I feel obliged to care for my nieces and nephews if anything happened to their parents? Why do I automatically think of home when I feel low? Why was I so upset by my mother leaving the family home to move to another country, even though I encouraged her to do so? Why is coming out to our parents so important still for lesbians and gay men? Why do many of us go home at Christmas? Why do some of us get covered in remorse if we forget a birthday? Why do we hate so much yet constantly try to create a 'family'? Why do we demand from other feminists and friends, some of the unparalleled acceptance that we once thought we had from our family? Why is the family such a safe place to love and hate, and yet also so unsafe? There are so many questions that beg an answer. That is what families do: leave us with endless questions.

In Conclusion: 'Who's still got Mr Bun's daughter?'

Families oppress women, that is what is said, therefore we

eliminate families. The impulse to revolutionary radicalism and the new feminist solution is pushed ahead, and behold, families and especially collective feminist and socialist alternatives should no longer oppress us. It is not working all that well. Have the new substitutes, which not only do not oppress women but can meet our needs as well, made us any happier? Sometimes, and sometimes not. The 'sometimes not' appears more often as feminists find households they put so much into disintegrating in the face of their desire for children or support or new sexual relations.

Somehow we need to split up the totality we call family. We must look at the good and the bad and the necessary and the unnecessary, which are not the same as each other. We are not always rational, totally dedicated feminists and/or socialists; we are also women and men trying to be feminists and socialists in an imperfect world where we hardly understand ourselves, let alone the families we come from. We spend our time trying to produce an imitation of something we have scarcely begun to analyse, fighting always the fact that our new forms often lack societal affirmation and therefore the symbolic significance conveyed on others by 'marriage'. We have been reluctant to give recognition to other aspects of the family which go beyond household forms and stereotypic oppression. We cannot confine other aspects to the therapeutic couch for ever. Nor can we flee the consequences of rejection like a bad raspberry pudding.

Sometimes it seems to me that those of us who have rejected the family have built into ourselves a button which says: 'Do not finish things. Reject others. Terminate and try again!' How many of us see our relationships through to a new level? Some try, many do not even bother. How can we learn, outside the family, the feelings of resentment and anger against dependency, and at the same time trust? We rebel against permanence, but we also want it. There are many needs which lurk around behind all our ideas and philosophies. We all want to be held and to hold. The family is the sentiment of society and of us all.

We have come a long way in our search for viable alternative ways of living. Yet the allure of our life-styles is not automatic. We are still a minority. But we have struggled, as feminists, with men, with household tasks, finances, house meetings, shared child-care and (we thought) responsibilities. In it we sort out an equality and a new life. We have made certain visible changes, and expectations *have* been altered. It has been the unseen which has been supremely difficult, and we have found that rhetoric is not enough. Reorganization of resources and tasks is not the same as living together. It seems to me that in all that we have done there has been little drastic alteration of structures. All that we have is more choice. We have dealt with the family as household. The future lies in dealing with family as a set of relationships.

8 The State, Welfare and Women's Dependence

FRAN BENNETT

Two examples show clearly that the state, the Welfare State, operates with a particular model of the family in mind. In this model, the man is assumed to be the breadwinner; he is expected to be in (or looking for) paid employment. The woman's primary role, on the other hand, is to care for dependants – the disabled, the elderly and children. The man's 'family wage' should support a wife and children too. The woman is assumed to be economically dependent on the man she lives with, if their relationship is (or is like) that of husband and wife:

A social worker one day suggests to one of his clients that she should invite her friend to come and share her flat. The client is a widow. For many years she has regularly helped her friend (male, disabled) with his housework, cooking and shopping. The social worker says that she will be able to help him more easily if he moves in with her. The widow agrees, and her friend moves in. Her widow's benefit, which she relies on, is immediately stopped, because she is accused of 'cohabiting' – living with a man as his wife.

A married woman with two young children is made redundant from her part-time job. Her husband's overtime working has also been reduced. They cannot afford the childminder's fees any more – and she should really be looking after the children at home anyway, her husband says to her. She goes down to the dole office to claim unemployment benefit. The official asks her if she is sure she can make adequate child-care arrangements in case she gets another job. She says no. The official tells her that her right to unemployment benefit is suspended: she is obviously not 'available for work', he says, if she has two children to look after.

The Welfare State treats the family as a unit, but a unit comprising different parts with different functions. Women are seen as financially dependent, but have no right of access to men's income – either from wages or benefits. Women are supposed to care, in private and with little help, for those who are physically dependent. In fact, the nature of the Welfare State's provision for the family depends to a large extent on its views about the role of women. When the Welfare State mentions 'the family', women are never far from its mind.

'Social security is about women', asserted a Labour Party Green Paper on Social Security in 1972, pointing to irrefutable statistics on the number of female pensioners who survived to draw their pensions years after year, and the growth in single-parent families, mostly headed by women, who lived on benefits.

Feminists needed no telling. We have never doubted that welfare is a crucial 'women's issue'. The campaign to introduce family allowances in the 1930s was led by feminists, as well as by eugenicists; the publication of Beveridge's Report in 1942, laying the foundations of the present Welfare State and social security system, was greeted with acclaim from many people, but with criticism from women's groups for its attitudes towards women.

We have often found ourselves in a dilemma as feminists, however. On the one hand, we argue that many of the debates on poverty, inequality and welfare in general are couched in terms which make women invisible or subsume them within the family. We have no idea how many women live in poverty, for example, since levels of income and wealth are measured by households and not by individuals. The disadvantages suffered by one-parent families are debated, with no recognition of the fact that many of these disadvantages arise simply because the vast majority of single parents are women. The arguments about whether people are better off out of work (the 'unemployment trap'), or whether they will lose in net income terms because of a gross wage rise (the 'poverty trap'), are conducted in ostensibly sex-neutral terms, but in fact usually relate only to married male workers with financially dependent families. No one seems to notice.

On the other hand, though, we would argue that welfare provision is not just a women's issue. Feminists have refused to see social policy as a soft option, marked 'for your eyes only' by economists, politicians and the male Left. We have seen the Welfare State, its organization and assumptions, as a central concern to both women and men, and as crucially related to both production and reproduction, economics and ideology.

Questions about 'women and the Welfare State', however, did not seem to loom large for the resurgent women's liberation movement in the late 1960s and early 1970s. *The Body Politic*,[1] perhaps the first collection of papers and articles to emerge self-consciously from the movement, contains only one article specifically about social security; and the fifth demand of the women's movement, calling for 'financial and legal independence' for women, was not adopted by a national conference until 1974. This is not to say that campaigns were not being waged, or that issues of income maintenance and state services were not being discussed at all. But it was the time of the equal pay strike at Ford's (1968), the disruption of the 'Miss World' contests (early 1970s), student demonstrations and the gay liberation marches. The urgent issues were women's right to work on equal terms with men, for the same pay; women's rediscovery of a personal and collective identity which conflicted with the stereotyped family roles of wife/mother/housewife; and women's exploration of the images of femininity and female sexuality, and what impact these models had on our lives.

Moreover, the movement had sprung from autonomous local groups with an emphasis on consciousness-raising rather than on formulating strategic demands on a national level. While there was an assumed (mutually beneficial) relationship between socialism and feminism, the connections were seen in terms of articulating a hitherto unrecognized form of oppression, and of initiating socialist (communal) ways of living in order to overcome it. Analysing and transforming the nature of paid and unpaid work, and the relationships between men and women – and, crucially, children – seemed more immediately relevant than developing a coherent feminist theory of the state and the family.

This is, of course, an incomplete picture. Women did come up against and concern themselves with the more repressive aspects of the state: women in prisons, police brutality, and 'sex snoopers' looking for signs of women claimants cohabiting with men. Priorities for debate and struggle were, in any case, changing as the women's liberation movement grew and widened its activities.

Several developments during the 1960s and early 1970s in fact made the state, and in particular the Welfare State, a central focus of writing, thinking and campaigning in the women's movement of the mid 1970s. There was a significant growth in public sector and white-collar employment, which drew in thousands of women workers; many were themselves active feminists, and wanted to discuss the content and concerns of their own jobs in the context of women's liberation. Married women's economic activity rates in general were increasing, too, with many more women thus having the experience of their own independent source of income. At the same time, there was a growth in the number of lone parents – partly through an increase in illegitimate births, but mainly through higher divorce and separation figures. Marriage could no longer be seen as a stable lifetime source of income. One-parent families tended to exist on benefits for longer than, for example, the unemployed, and so, in some areas, formed the nucleus of Claimants' Unions as well as the focus of their struggles.

Given its initial connections with the Left, too, the women's liberation movement could not fail to be influenced by the debates going on within the Left in the 1970s about the role of the state. Many active feminists were themselves also members of Left groups, and wanted to bring a feminist perspective to bear on the discussions about the state's economic and ideological functions, and its relationship with capitalist production, and – they said increasingly loudly – reproduction. Women academics were also starting to develop ideas about women and the family in the fields of social policy; Hilary Land wrote an article called 'Women: Supporters or Supported?',[2] examining the way in which women were seen by the state as simultaneously dependent and themselves the major carers for dependants within the family.

It is now ten years since the first national women's movement campaign on a welfare issue. The Tory Government's tax credit scheme, elaborated in 1972, would have (among other things) transferred cash support for children from mothers to fathers. Even though the sums involved in family allowances were minimal, the women's movement saw the scheme as a threat to the only source of independent income which some women had, and fought vigorously against it. The scheme, in that form at least, was abandoned; and the child-benefit scheme, introduced later by a Labour Government, kept the benefit in the hands of mothers. But the debate around the Tories' attempt to hijack family allowances first raised in a concrete form the issues of an independent income for women, what form that income should take, and for what reason it should be given – all of which would be central for the women's movement in the later 1970s.

Somehow or other, the more theoretical discussions about 'welfare' issues in the women's liberation movement of the 1970s always seemed to return to the same things: the sexual division of labour; the contribution of housework and child-care to the smooth running of either the economy or men; and whether this domestic labour should be either financially rewarded in its own right, shared more equally between the sexes, or withdrawn from men by women. These themes were central, despite any differences of political perspective or vocabulary between the various feminist groups.

There were differences, of course. Some feminists concentrated on teasing out the reasons why the Welfare State operated as it did in relation to women; others on prescribing solutions to liberate women from their dependent role. The Marxist feminists who emphasized analysis of the interest which the state had in maintaining women's dependence were often described as having a 'functionalist' view. In other words, they saw the Welfare State as having been designed with a clear purpose in mind: to serve the interests of capitalism by regulating domestic life. If women were needed in production, their role in the reproduction of the workforce for capital must not be jeopardized as a result. 'Welfare provision . . . operates in a more subtle and in some ways a more coercive fashion to keep women to their primary task as adults. This is the task of reproducing the workforce.'[3] Welfare provision assumes and reinforces women's economic dependence on men, who in turn are made more dependent on waged labour. There ensued a heated, esoteric and in the end rather sterile debate on the academic Left about whether domestic work was 'productive' or not – the domestic labour debate, as it was known.

Other Marxist feminists were identified more with the solutions which they proposed – such as the 'Wages for Housework' campaign. 'Wages for Housework' feminists saw themselves as linked with community struggles rather than with the organized Labour Movement, de-emphasized women's role in the paid labour force, and were particularly influenced by feminists in Italy in the late 1960s and their analysis of the 'material foundation for sisterhood' which housework provided. As their name implies, 'Wages for Housework' (WFH) saw women as part of the working class – the only unpaid part – whose class position, and economic and sexual choices, would be clarified if women were given a wage for domestic work. (They usually made no distinction between servicing another independent adult – that is, housework – and caring for dependent children.) The WFH position implied a different attitude to the state from that of other Marxist feminists: the state could be enlisted to enhance women's freedom, and the income it was supposed to guarantee would be a consciousness-raising tool in itself: 'Until housework is clearly seen as work and commands a wage, our entire nature is identified with it, and our struggles against it are harder to win.'[4]

Successive campaigns for 'Wages for Housework' to be accepted as one of the demands of the women's liberation movement were always defeated at national Women's Liberation Movement Conferences during the 1970s. But both 'Wages for Housework' groups and other Marxist feminists saw themselves as arguing from within the women's movement. What they had in common was a desire to explore the relationship between women's oppression by capitalism and by men, and how the state aided and abetted both – however different their conclusions and solutions might be to the problem.

But the women's movement was also having to sort out its attitudes to other campaigns and groups with their own programmes and ideas about welfare. The most important of these – in terms of the political orientation of the Women's Liberation Movement, rather than their own influence and power – were the Claimants' Union movement and the 'poverty lobby'. These were often seen as representing respectively the 'revolutionary' and 'reformist' wings of the small group of people working on ideas of how to change the Welfare State for the better.

Claimants' Unions were small local groups of social security claimants who tried to combat the isolating experience of claiming benefits by getting together to sort out problems and confront the authorities collectively. But the national Claimants' Union movement was, in fact, decreasing in membership numbers and political optimism throughout the 1970s. Its major long-term demand has always been for a 'guaranteed minimum income' (GMI) to be paid to all, in or out of employment, replacing most or all social security benefits and allowances. The interesting point about this demand from the point of view of the women's movement was that the GMI would be paid on an individual basis – rather than to men as breadwinners for the family.

In 1977, the national Women's Liberation Movement Conference passed a resolution calling for 'a GMI as of right with clear legal entitlement' for 'every individual person whether in or out of employment'. The Claimants' Unions were probably more concerned with undermining the 'social control which the wages system imposes on the whole of the working class'[5] than in women's liberation; but they claimed that the GMI would resolve the question of, 'Independence from whom?' for women, because it would unite women working at home unpaid, low-paid women, and women claiming benefits. But the GMI (unlike wages for housework) was seen more as a means of enforcing improvement in women's wages and conditions of paid work than as a specific payment for the work of housework and child-care.

Despite the superficially attractive nature of the GMI as a radical demand, however, many feminists were suspicious. They saw it as an over-simplified and probably unattainable solution to the complex problem of the relationship between the wages system and domestic labour. As with 'Wages for Housework', money by itself could not be the answer. Instead of forcing employers to improve paid work for women, a GMI might encourage them to go on paying low wages, knowing that women had access to other income in any case. And despite the conference's call for financial and legal independence for women, most feminists were concerned that a demand for economic compensation alone would detract from demands for socialized child-care, equal access to waged work for women, and a redistribution of waged and domestic labour between the sexes. Both wages for housework and the GMI were claimed by their supporters to give women a 'choice' about whether to do paid work or not; if they had a sufficient income anyway, second jobs would have to be made much more attractive by employers.

But critics of this easy conclusion argued that 'choice' is a very slippery concept in the context of women's work, given the prevailing ideological pressures on women; and that the real problem is the lack of choice which women have about domestic labour. Being paid a wage for doing it would not change this situation. They were also critical of the reliance on the state to provide a guarantee of income regardless of employment status and argued that the form of benefit given, not just the fact of it, was important. A GMI could not be a short cut to the transformation of either capitalism and the wages system, or patriarchy and the sexual division of labour. To expect the Welfare State, and an income received from it, to be the engine of revolution for women by itself was to attack the wrong target with the wrong strategy.

The 'poverty lobby', emerging into prominence at about the same time as the women's movement, was also in a permanently uneasy relationship with the Claimants' Unions and other GMI enthusiasts. This was partly due to its distinctive political background – as the largely middle-class inheritors of the

Fabian tradition of gradual social reform – and partly to its chosen context of political activity. The poverty groups, chief among them the Child Poverty Action Group (CPAG), concentrated on parliamentary persuasion first and foremost, pioneering the 'new' pressure group lobbying of government and opposition alike, and the production of informed research and polemic. Unlike the Claimants' Union movement, they had no direct constituent group of 'genuine claimants', and did not pretend to be searching for new forms of democratic participation or collective struggle against the state. They were, moreover, identified with a 'pro-family' approach to some extent, which the women's movement (rightly) regarded with some suspicion. There was, at best, an arm's-length relationship between the two.

Feminists were trying to emphasize what interests women had in common as a basis for action. The poverty lobby was simultaneously stressing the potentially positive impact which a 'classless' family lobby would have on traditional class loyalties and politics. Feminists were apprehensive that women's specific interests would get lost as usual under the banner of the interests of the family unit.

Of course, some women in the poverty groups were also active feminists; and the interests of the women's movement and the poverty lobby could, and did, converge on occasions. Frank Field, ex-director of CPAG, has complained that these occasions were mainly defensive and negative campaigns. (See, for example, his recent book *The Politics of Poverty*.) [6] They were none the less important, especially given the tendency of welfare provision to remain in place and unchanged, once it has been introduced. We have managed to avoid implementing some dubious proposals – the Tory tax credit scheme having already been mentioned. Another example was the means-tested 'one-parent family benefit' proposed by the Finer Report in 1974.

But the latter example does illustrate the problems of

defensive unity. Neither the poverty lobby nor feminists wanted yet another degrading means-tested benefit – this time specifically for one-parent families – to be introduced. Both were against introducing a new benefit which, once again, relied heavily on the cohabitation rule, whereby women on certain benefits have to give them up, and rely instead on the man with whom they are found to be 'living together as husband and wife'. To the poverty lobby, the policing of the cohabitation rule, involving 'snooping', intrusive questions and accusations of fraud, is unacceptable. To the women's movement, the cohabitation rule implies that a heterosexual relationship must and should involve financial dependence (or maintenance in return for sexual and other services). Women deprived of money to live on are forced to rely on a man for economic support. But the rejection of the Finer Report's proposal (which was also refused by the government) leaves us with no provision for single parents – apart from widows – other than the present derisory supplementary benefit. And supplementary benefit is all the things which were objected to in the proposed one-parent family benefit; that is, it is not only means-tested, but also comes with a cohabitation rule attached.

The idea of an income as of right for women – and lone parents in particular – has always seemed threatening to a conservative or traditionalist view of the family which stresses the natural, wholesome goodness of the nuclear family in its idealized, rigid form. It is not only feminists who have sensed the potential of a demand for women to be able to be economically independent of men. Workers in Women's Aid refuges in the 1970s discovered that one in five separated wives were better off on supplementary benefit than they had been when they were married. For this situation to be deliberately engineered would have been unthinkable for most politicians, especially on the Right. If women were able to survive economically on their own, that might tempt them out of the nuclear family set-up, which was suddenly seen as a fragile structure, rather than the firm and unchanging bedrock of society. Indeed, if they were to receive an income, however small, when they were married, that might also undermine the different family responsibilities of both sexes: the women might no longer feel dependent on the men, and the men might no longer want to provide for their wives and children.

Feminism became more explicit about the economic dependence and hidden poverty of married women in the late 1970s, too. Much use was made of a survey by a women's magazine which showed that men's wage rises were not feeding through to increased housekeeping money. The Campaign for Financial and Legal Independence and the YBA Wife? campaign were set up within the women's movement. Both emphasized that measuring joint incomes of couples gave no real clue to what standard of living the woman enjoyed – or, more often, endured. The accusations of 'women's libbers' enticing women away from husband and children to a life of luxury on benefits became louder. (This was despite the continuing criticisms by Women's Aid workers and other feminists of the totally inadequate benefit provision for women with children on their own.) In November 1980, the Chancellor of the Exchequer, Geoffrey Howe, asked rhetorically about child benefit: 'Does the mother feel greater independence because she is not dependent on the father for the children's support? Does the father feel less need to provide as much for the housekeeping and for the children?'[7] Obviously an independent income for women, whether inside or outside marriage, was a real threat.

Such reactions are interesting, because they betray an implicit view that it is really financial need which is necessary to bind many women to the family home (and incidentally men to the shop floor). They are, perhaps, as much a response to the growing economic independence of women as to the women's movement itself. Indeed, often feminists who had left their husbands found it difficult to separate in their own minds the factors making their departure possible: was it the consciousness-raising which pushed me, or did I jump because I knew that economic survival (alone or with children) was possible? The statements which sometimes emerged from the women's liberation movement of the 1970s, about the consciousness-raising potential of an income derived from the state or from wages rather than from men, have in some ways been merely the other side of the coin from those made by the pro-family Right in different language. In both cases, it was assumed that women's financial dependence was necessary for the smooth functioning of 'civilization as we know it' – that is, capitalism and the male-dominated nuclear family. In both cases, women's financial independence was seen as a potent catalyst for change. The Right feared such change as a threat, whereas the women's liberation movement welcomed it as an opportunity. Did both perhaps exaggerate its power?

As in other areas of feminist activity, it has not been possible to define one particular view as that of 'the' women's liberation movement; nor has any group put itself forward as having the right to represent the women's movement view on welfare. But, in the last few years, with the production of so many consultative and discussion documents about changes to benefit provision which affect women, some groups within the movement have increasingly believed that it is essential to put forward a feminist viewpoint to government and other bodies. Thus, for example, both the Campaign for Financial and Legal Independence and ROW (Rights of Women, a group of feminist legal workers) wrote responses to the government's review of the supplementary benefits scheme during 1978–80. The review was, in the main, concerned with reducing discretion within the supplementary benefits scheme, and introducing clearer legal rules at no extra cost. Claimants would have a legal right to each bit of supplementary benefit which they qualified for, but instead of judgements being made by civil servants, there would be strict regulations about who qualified for what and who did not qualify at all. But the review was also carried out under the shadow of an EEC directive, which in 1978 gave member states six years to implement some legislative reforms as a move towards equality of treatment between men and women in the field of social security. This was the area which feminists concentrated on in particular.

ROW, for example, argued for 'disaggregation' of supplementary benefit, meaning that it should be awarded to each individual, whether in a heterosexual couple or not, rather than to the man for himself and his wife or woman cohabitee. At present, supplementary benefit is given to an 'assessment unit' which, where applicable, consists of man, female sexual partner and any dependent children; any resources which this unit has are 'aggregated' (added together) for means-testing purposes, and any benefit is given to the man for all of them. That is, the state enforces its model of marriage, of women's dependence on men, for *all* heterosexual households, even where there is no marriage context.

ROW argued that this assumed an existing share-out of finances which did not necessarily occur; and that it then ensured and enforced female economic dependence. ROW called for 'disaggregation now', with benefits being assessed and paid individually, regardless of any savings or income which the other partner has. Neither partner should be forced to depend on the other. No cohabitation rule would therefore be necessary.

However, disaggregation was obviously an idea whose time – as far as the government was concerned – had not yet come. They threw up their hands in horror at the increase in the numbers of people claiming supplementary benefit which this move would represent, and especially at the vision of wealthy husbands' wives trooping down to the Department of Health and Social Security to collect their supplementary benefit every week. R O W said that they thought this weekly exodus unlikely, and that in any case, any inequality thus created should be dealt with through the taxation system instead. After all, few people any longer feel that there is anything wrong about a sixteen-year-old drawing benefit regardless of the wealth or poverty of his or her parents; why should not wives and female cohabitees have 'disaggregation now' as well?

It is worth noting that several feminist demands about an independent income for women have been countered, as was this one, by arguments such as the above, which stress their potential impact on class inequality. (A more recent example, described in greater detail later, has been the debate on the government's Green Paper on the Taxation of Husband and Wife.) But, in the meantime, the government's 'solution' to the discrimination inherent in a man's right to claim benefit for both himself and his female partner was to suggest – and legislate for – a right, in 'role reversal' situations, for the woman to claim for both instead. The couple's resources would continue to be aggregated for means-testing, and benefit would continue to be given to one partner for the other's needs as well. There was to be no division of the assumed economic unit of the couple into separate and independent individuals.

The result is that, from 1983/4, if the woman has been the 'main breadwinner' for the previous six months, she can claim supplementary benefit for herself and the man she lives with too. And, in a similar move, if she is the full-time worker in a couple, and the man is not (for a good, and long-term, reason), they can claim family income supplement as an addition to her low earnings if they have a child or children.

The latter is certainly an improvement on the current situation, in which two-parent families can claim family income supplement only if the male partner is working full-time. But, as with the change in supplementary benefit rules, there is ultimately no challenge to the idea of the married or cohabiting couple as a private, caring, sharing unit; there is merely a concession to the reality of 'role reversal' in a few, untypical couples. (Role reversal couples are anyway treated very well already – by an anomalous quirk – under the tax system in this country.) The supplementary benefit and family income supplement rule changes were forced on the government, in any case, to meet the requirements of the 1978 EEC directive on social security and equal treatment; and Section 51 of the Sex Discrimination Act (which exempts government legislation passed before 1975, and later amendments to that legislation, from the anti-discrimination requirements) escapes unscathed. So most of the discrimination in the social security system can be left unchanged.

For example, the directive does not appear to cover benefits unrelated to paid work (though feminists, among others, are disputing the interpretation of this exemption). This means that two of the most notoriously discriminatory benefits – housewives' non-contributory invalidity pension and invalid care allowance – do not have to be changed at all to comply with Common Market law.

The housewives' non-contributory invalidity pension is, in effect, 'wages for (non)-housework', since a disabled married or cohabiting woman must prove that she is incapable of performing 'normal household duties' properly before she can get the benefit. Anyone else who claims non-contributory invalidity pension has only got to prove that they are incapable of doing paid employment. The invalid care allowance rules represent, on the other hand, an assertion that a married or cohabiting woman's natural, unpaid function is to care for others. It is an allowance available to everyone (except married or cohabiting women) who cares for a disabled person for at least thirty-five hours a week, and has little or no income from earnings.

The arguments on extending invalid care allowance eligibility to these women provide an interesting study for feminists, who have joined with the disability groups in pressing for extension. Most full-time 'community care' for the disabled and elderly is in fact provided by women, as the Equal Opportunities Commission (EOC) has graphically proved. Recent Policy Studies Institute research has estimated that one in two women will be involved in caring for elderly or disabled parents at some time in her life.[8] This means that the cost of extending invalid care allowance is significant. But this is not the government's primary reason for refusing to concede to the growing pressure. If invalid care allowance were extended to married and cohabiting women, the government might argue, what would be the logical objection to a payment to women living with men for looking after children at home? And back we are to the questions of an independent income for women.

Feminists have not argued against the extension of invalid care allowance on the grounds that this would be paying women to stay at home. Yet we would expect these arguments to be advanced automatically if the government suggested wages for full-time child-care by mothers. The reasoning may be that thousands of women are caring for the disabled at home anyway, with or without an income for doing it; and that many women who care for the disabled would be of the age-group least likely to wish to return to paid employment. And it would obviously be ridiculous to oppose the extension of invalid care allowance when everyone else – apart from most women – is paid to stay at home if they care for a disabled person. 'Care' in this situation is also likely to mean a more full-time occupation than child-care. But the implications above do not seem to have been discussed in the women's movement. Neither have we said openly that an income for individual carers at home reduces the pressure for collective services. Yet both these points would, I am sure, have been raised and argued about if the benefit payments were to have been made for full-time child-care.

Far from providing a 'meal ticket for life', it appears in the case of invalid care allowance that marriage (or indeed cohabitation) permanently removes the woman's right to luncheon vouchers. The EOC highlighted this in their publicity campaign on invalid care allowance in various women's magazines, which showed a marriage service, with the priest asking whether the bride also promised to give up her right to invalid care allowance. Marriage for men, on the other hand, does provide a real and immediate financial benefit, in the form of the married man's tax allowance. This allowance, originally introduced to compensate men for the supposed financial burden of supporting a wife, is given to all married men, and is worth about £5 a week to most at the moment. The calls for its abolition have been almost unanimous, and have come from a wide range of organizations, such as the poverty lobby, feminist groups and the old-style women's organizations as well.

The government suggested abolishing the married man's tax allowance in a recent Green Paper, as one of a number of possible reforms to the taxation system as it affects married couples. It has now got cold feet. The Green Paper had, in any case, made clear that the government favoured retaining the status quo, with a continued premium on marriage for men, and a continued pattern of joint rather than individual taxation. The husband would continue to be responsible for the payment of tax on his wife's income in law; and men who had 'gone through a marriage ceremony more recently than a divorce'[9] would continue to benefit to the tune of £5 a week or more. In the face of so many calls for the abolition of the married man's tax allowance, and for individuals to be responsible for their own tax affairs, the government has redoubled its efforts. Government ministers emphasize the number of people who would lose out, and stress the effects on low-income couples and men with non-earning wives.

The issues which are being linked by the government and its

opponents are financial independence for women, child support and family poverty. In other words, if the married man's tax allowance were abolished, every adult could be taxed individually, regardless of sex or marital status. If the resources raised from married men ($£2-£3$ billion) were redirected, child benefit could be doubled. This would help families with children, who are often most at risk of being in poverty. Older couples with a non-earning wife are among the better-off section of the population on average.

These linked issues can lead to a formidable alliance of groups and campaigns which can, for once, fight for something which enhances women's independent status while also providing more support for the family. The coincidence of interests has been seized upon with relief, as it was when child benefit was introduced in 1977. Thus the Study Commission for the Family (an independent research unit set up a few years ago), several trade unions and the Child Poverty Action Group can arrive at the same conclusions – though by a different route – as the National Council for Civil Liberties (influenced by its active Rights for Women Unit) and the Equal Opportunities Commission.

However, the war of words over the taxation of married couples has also resulted in some stranger bedfellows. Rights of Women (see page 202) and the Trades Union Congress, for example, concur in calling for the abolition of the married man's tax allowance and the introduction of individually based taxation; but they then both suggest that the additional resources thus generated should be used to increase the personal tax allowance (for every individual) as a priority, rather than to increase child benefit. Their motivations and the interest groups they are protecting are, of course, very different; but the coincidence of their views perhaps sheds light on some important dilemmas facing the women's movement too.

The Trades Union Congress is responding to a gut reaction

from some of its middle-aged, male, married trade union leaders, who probably have non-earning wives. They are also (coincidentally, of course!) very sensitive to the fact that abolishing the married man's tax allowance would lower the tax threshold for a large group of workers, and they fear that this would be politically unpopular. ROW is defending the principle of an independent income for women as its first priority, and pointing out that child benefit is, of course, an income for children, which many women would not benefit from; they stress that the separate needs of women are being hidden under the label of children's needs by the demand for higher child benefit. They would prefer to see any additional resources going into a higher personal tax allowance, to enhance the net earnings of women, whose gross earnings are usually so much lower than men's.

The Trades Union Congress's viewpoint highlights the tightrope which feminists working for changes in benefits walk: on the one hand, advocating financial independence for women, and on the other, trying not to penalize women who are, in fact, dependent upon men at present. Non-earning full-time housewives will not have any income to offset against their individual tax allowance, and their husbands will lose £5 a week, if the married man's tax allowance is abolished. If they have no dependent children, they will gain nothing either from the proposed increase in child benefit. This is generally thought acceptable by some feminists, and by the poverty lobby, who argue that these are generally better-off couples anyway. They would argue that women in this situation would be better served by being able to 'sign on' as available for paid work, and claim their own unemployment benefit; though the unemployment benefit rules would have to be changed so that women who had not had a paid job for a long time could still get benefit. (This is, in fact, what already happens under the Swedish social insurance system.)[10]

ROW's position exposes another sensitive spot for feminists, who have always fought for and welcomed the payment of child benefit (formerly family allowances) to mothers for their children. It is true, however, that payment to the mother was argued for on the basis of women's dependent status, but that it does not provide the solution to the problem of an independent income for women. Child benefit gives women no money for their own needs at all; in fact, it can be seen as confirming the division of responsibility within the family, and as reinforcing women's role as devoted and unselfish carers who (unlike men) can be trusted to put children's needs before their own.

But when we demand an independent income for women, we must examine the necessary practical questions about the form and purpose of such an income. Financial independence for women is still an essential demand for the women's liberation movement. Raising it in the context of most discussions on social security leads to fundamental questions about the relationship of paid to unpaid work – and about the division of these between the sexes – which are usually completely ignored; and seeking an answer to them leads directly towards radical change both in the benefits system and beyond.

Yet, as the volume of feminist work in the field of social security builds up, so does our awareness of the more detailed and awkward problems behind the slogans such as, 'Financial independence for women', or, 'Disaggregation now'. For example: what kind of benefit, given under what conditions, do we want for women who are not in paid work at present? Any benefits based on employment status (such as the present contributory national insurance benefits like unemployment and sickness benefit) inevitably privilege those with a full-time, unbroken work and earnings record – that is, primarily men. On the other hand, extending the right to claim supplementary benefit to married or cohabiting women as individuals would involve a massive expansion of intrusive means-testing.

If the receipt of benefit were conditional on women being available for paid work, regardless of domestic responsibilities, it has been argued, this would reinforce the privileged status already given to paid employment, and the systematic relegation of domestic labour to a lower position. If it were, instead, given to women unconditionally if they had domestic responsibilities (as it is for single parents at present, in fact), feminists would see it as merely another form of 'Wages for Housework', or at least paying women to stay at home. (Eleanor Rathbone, who campaigned for family allowances, used to call this 'endowment of motherhood'. There have been many recent letters in the national papers calling for women who look after children at home full-time to get an allowance of their own.)

One solution proposed to this dilemma has been the introduction of a taxable 'family responsibility payment', paid as an addition to child benefit to someone with responsibility for children (or other dependants) whether the carer was in or out of paid employment. (Because it is taxable, rather than being withdrawn entirely on receipt of any earnings, it is argued that this would minimize any disincentive effects to taking a paid job as well; while it would give at least some income of their own to women carers at home.) This proposal seems to be gaining ground, and has been put forward by the CPAG as a possible development parallel to the abolition of the married man's tax allowance (see pages 207–9). But critics point out that, in practical terms, the allowance would probably not be set at a high enough level to replace earnings adequately. There is also a suspicion that it would hinder more radical moves towards redistributing paid and domestic labour between men and women, because in most cases it would be seen as a payment to mothers, not to parents of either sex.

There is also a deepening consciousness in the women's movement of the limitations placed on Welfare State reforms by the wages system as it works at present. There has been a spate of feminist work recently on the construction of gender and the subordination of women in the workplace, including historical studies of men's assertion of the right to earn a 'family wage' which is sufficiently high to maintain a dependent wife and children. The ideology of the family wage sets powerful boundaries on the revolutionary consciousness-raising potential of an independent income for women. Feminist research and writing in the fields of education, language and ideology have made it impossible to make the simple assertion (as 'Wages for Housework' did in 1978): 'the power relationship between men and women . . . is based on money'.[11] We emphasize more the deeply ingrained feelings of inferiority into which women are socialized. We are more aware of these limitations today than in the early years of the women's movement. And, after twenty years in which the proportion of women with dependent children who are in paid employment has doubled, we must also be more conscious of new areas of vulnerability for women – such as the increasing impact of the 'double shift' with all its accompanying stresses. Financial independence, total or partial, has not in many cases made an enormous amount of difference to the lived reality of many women's lives; although no one would seek to deny the effect which some income of our own has on women's expectations and feelings of confidence.

In some ways, there seems to be a backlash against women's liberation. So we find ourselves, as feminists, paradoxically emphasizing the reality of the continuing economic dependence of women, and in some cases advocating a continued expectation of financial support by women from men. A recently formed and very effective pressure group, for example, is the Campaign for Justice in Divorce, which campaigns on behalf of men who are supporting two families because of a previous divorce and subsequent remarriage. It argues that marriage should not be seen any longer as a source of life-long financial support for women. In retaliation against the campaign's declarations that equality for women has already been achieved, we have been forced to stress women's continuing dependence on men – exactly the assumption which we have been criticizing for years in the social security system. We have also wondered whether we are letting men off the hook too lightly – for example, if by calling for a guaranteed income from the state for one-parent families, men can more easily absent themselves from any responsibilities.

Despite this complexity the women's movement can look back on its work around the state, welfare and women's dependence, and establish some principles which have guided us from the beginning, but have been refined and sharpened over the last fifteen years. We are calling for an independent income for women – but not at any price. We are aware of the potential of financial independence for women's liberation – without exaggerating its potential as a strategy by itself. We want a social security system which recognizes the value of domestic labour – without creating inducements to women to stay at home full-time. We want a benefits system which takes account of social and economic changes and deliberately encourages further change in the power relations between men and women and the sexual division of labour – but we also want the state to compensate, where necessary, for women's continuing inequality and dependence. Is it too much to ask?

Notes and References

1. M. Wandor (ed.), *The Body Politic*, Stage 1, 1972.
2. Hilary Land, 'Women: Supporters or Supported?', in D. Leonard Barker and S. Allen (eds.), *Sexual Divisions in Society*, Tavistock Publications, London, 1978.
3. Elizabeth Wilson, *Women and the Welfare State*, Tavistock Publications, London, 1977.
4. Maria della Costa and Selma James, *The Power of Women and the Subversion of the Community*, Falling Wall Press, Bristol, 1975.

5. See *Scarlet Women*, Issue 8, August 1978.
6. Frank Field, *The Politics of Poverty*, Heinemann Educational Books, London, 1982.
7. At a meeting of the Family Forum, grouping organizations concerned with the interests of families. Quoted in Anna Coote and Beatrix Campbell, *Sweet Freedom: The Struggle for Women's Liberation*, Picador, London, 1982.
8. Muriel Nissel and Lucy Bonnerjea, *Family Care of the Handicapped and of the Elderly: Who Pays?*, Policy Studies Institute Report No. 602, London, 1982.
9. Quoted in Coote and Campbell, *Sweet Freedom*.
10. See Hilda Scott, *Sweden's Right to be Human*, Allison and Busby, London, 1982.
11. See *Scarlet Women*, Issue No. 8, August 1978.

*No Turning Back – Thatcherism,
the Family and the Future*

LYNNE SEGAL

'It's all right for the blokes, isn't it?' I overheard one working-
class woman say to another while waiting at the Family Planning
clinic, each with her new baby. Most women are still marrying
and having children, and living, though now for only a part of
their lives, in nuclear families – families where their husbands
must support them and their children, while they are devoted
to child-care. And in this situation the blokes *are*, on the whole,
better cared for, less isolated, less harassed and less vulnerable
to depression and anxiety than their wives. Though children are
leaving home sooner, and women who now have fewer children
are inevitably less home based, that image of the husband out at
work and the wife at home with her young baby embodies the
idea of family life – like an eternal freeze frame from the video
of life.

It survives in our minds, and though for increasingly shorter
periods, in most of our lives. It survives, though family groups
are far more diverse and less stable nowadays, with or without a
marriage certificate. It survives even though the number of
people marrying has shown a downward trend in the last ten
years, despite the sixfold increase in divorce since 1961, despite
'illegitimate' births increasing to 12 per cent of all births, and
despite the significant increase in single parents, cohabitation
and people living alone. Its survival remains at the heart of
women's continuing subordination to men.

What are the prospects for change? It is always hard to
distinguish between what is happening in the world, like changes
in employment, social policy, the choices we have been able to

make in our lives, and prevalent myths and ideologies. We are living out the ideologies, striving to be good wives or mothers, at the same time as social change exacerbates their contradictions; unemployment or denial of benefit increases family tension. So, though family life has been changing more rapidly than ever in recent years, it is still popularly seen as based on 'eternal verities', 'biological imperatives' and natural laws. Changing family forms are mostly ignored, denied or registered with alarm, and sometimes apprehended with a strange mixture of all three. Only a radical minority of feminists and some socialists are likely to confront change as a challenge to enrich our lives in the future.

Ferdinand Mount, a new policy advisor and speech writer for Margaret Thatcher, for example, writes of the timeless 'duties of care prescribed [for women] by the biological ethic' in the 'natural' family.[1] While the policy- and speech-maker herself warns us that the 'permissive society', with its 'emphasis on self-improvement', has been of no benefit to women.[2] The sexual reforms of the 1960s, which some women struggled for – easier contraception, abortion and divorce, limited gay rights and greater tolerance towards sexuality outside of marriage – are presented as a threat to women, undermining the security and respect of 'the family'. Even the expansion of welfare services, on this view, becomes a threat to the 'privacy and independence' of the family, a threat to women's biological right to the sacrifice of self (as distinct from her acquired need for self-fulfilment!) 'It is women who have lost most,' the paternalistic sages of the Right say to frighten us, while denying the existence of continued sexual inequality. 'The battle for women's rights has been largely won,' Thatcher tells us.[3] The conservative message is that the old ideals of marriage and the family, women know, have not really changed. But to the extent that they *have* changed, it is women who have suffered. Feminists need to abandon earlier critiques of sexual repression, marriage and the family – indeed, according to current conservative convention, they largely have.

Examining women's lives today suggests a more complex story. There have been, for instance, both advantages and disadvantages as liberal reforms have accompanied rapid changes in our lives in the last two decades. More accessible contraception and abortion remove the nightmare of illegal abortion and some of the fear of sex for women. We cannot afford to forget just how tragic many women's lives used to be, facing, chronically fearing, or attempting to remove unwanted pregnancy before abortion law reforms. Thousands of women died and still die in countries where abortion remains illegal. Thousands of women were victimized as unmarried mothers. The contradictions surrounding the acceptable expression of young women's sexuality in the 1950s as seductive, saucy and knowing while simultaneously virginal, vulnerable and ignorant, were truly crippling. 'My idea of hell is to be young again,' writes Marge Piercy in her latest novel, where she recalls reaching adulthood in the 1950s, describing the deadly dangerous sexual encounters of women at that time.[4] 'I believe in being honest with men,' her heroine informs her mother, only to hear: 'You poor idiot. Stick with that line and you'll end up raped and dead in a ditch with your throat slit.'[5] A fate one of her characters narrowly escapes, only to end up dead from a backstreet abortion.

Married women's relatively greater economic independence, drawn increasingly into the workforce in the 1960s – if only in part-time and sporadic work – did make it easier for some of them to leave unhappy or violent marriages, just as it made it easier for some of them to seek greater equality in the home. Before the late 1960s, there was almost no talk of men sharing housework or child-care. But since that time the idea that men *should* share, or 'help with' domestic tasks has steadily grown, though the reality of men's contribution rarely matches any goal of equality.

Back in 1972, Jessie Bernard had spoken of the 'two marriages' in every marriage, where the psychological costs for
wives in marriage were far greater and the benefits far fewer.[6]
On every measure of stress from physical to mental ill health,
wives suffered more than their husbands, and more than single
women, though working wives showed fewer symptoms of
psychological disturbance than did full-time housewives.
Married men were far healthier than single men, but single
women suffered the least stress of all. Higher symptoms of
stress in married women are also reported in subsequent similar
studies in both the United States and Britain.[7] So it is known
that married women fare less well out of marriage than do men,
which is no doubt one reason for the American evidence of a
correlation between working wives and divorce.[8] The greater
the independence of women, it would seem, the less stable is
marriage. Divorce statistics show that in 1980 in England and
Wales 71 per cent of petitions were filed by wives.[9] While it is
true that women may be the ones forced into legal action because
of their need for maintenance for themselves or their children,
it is nevertheless also true that only 3 per cent of divorces were
filed on the grounds of desertion (compared to 8 per cent in
1972), while the commonest ground cited, up 15 per cent from
1972, was the unacceptable behaviour of spouses. Greater
economic freedom, combined with easier divorce, which has
enabled at least a significant number of women to leave unhappy marriages, is, despite Thatcher, hardly something which
inevitably fails to benefit women; any more than the increasing
numbers of women who cohabit, live alone or in other com-
binations, necessarily and inevitably indicate a deteriorating
situation for women.

And yet there are many ways in which women's situation
generally has not improved, indeed, in which women would
seem to be worse off. As the number of single parents increases,
90 per cent of them women, so the number of women and

children who live in poverty increases. In the same way, with
the increase in the number of people who live alone (the other
fastest growing household type, particularly among the elderly),
the number of women who live impoverished and isolated also
increases. Partly because they live longer, but also because they
are typically younger than their husbands, there are many more
elderly women who live alone. For example, between 1979 and
1980 there were three times the number of elderly women
living alone as men.[10] The loneliness and poverty of elderly
people has been steadily increasing in recent years, as many
of them will have no living children, and nearly all now
have fewer children, and children who are more dispersed than
ever before. Many older people cannot be cared for by relatives in the family, however much that may suit Tory budget
cuts. In 1980, one third of the elderly had no surviving children.[11]

Other problems associated with the needs and care of the
elderly expose the particular strains on women in families today.
It is well known that family care of the elderly, when it can be
provided, is provided overwhelmingly by women in families.
Yet although women must withdraw from paid work or restrict
their paid work, as well as restrict their holiday and leisure
time, married women can receive no financial assistance from
the state. They are ineligible for the invalid tax allowance. In
fact, 67 per cent of married women between forty-five and
fifty-nine work outside the home, and roughly a quarter of
them are also caring for an elderly or infirm relative, often
combining the two tasks with considerable strain and difficulty.[12]

More generally, despite the fact that husbands and wives
now believe that men and women *should* share household chores,
surveys have shown repeatedly that the majority of housework
is still performed by women. This is even so in households
where husbands and wives work for the same amount of time

outside the home. For instance, Penny Mansfield's recent survey of over fifty families where husbands and wives both worked full time, revealed that wives still did almost all the washing, cleaning and cooking after work, while men did little more than help with the shopping, washing up and making the beds.[13] Similar studies reveal how very little has changed in the household, and that husbands of working wives do almost as little housework as husbands of full-time housewives.[14]

This is the problem with Betty Friedan's fantasy of the 'second stage' of feminism.[15] In this stage, she assures us, from careful observation of her son, fathers will share the 'joys and burdens' of child-care and home-making; unions and industry will give priority to *men's* demands for shorter and flexible working hours; and, if we seriously think we can leave it to men to make these demands, pigs will fly. It is not so much Friedan's vision which is wrong, as her refusal to accept what, of course, she must know of men's resistance to change. That is the reason we are *not* yet in any 'second stage', but women are still inevitably confronting men, and demanding they confront each other, at every turn. This is not to deny that there are some men, affected by feminism, who have been through a lot, and changed a lot. This has meant not only changing their personal relations with each other, and with women and children, but confronting their own hostility and competitiveness towards women. And it has meant taking *public* responsibility for challenging male power and privilege, and for reassessing the negative aspects of masculinity. But such men are still very much the exception – even if the exception that can encourage our hopes of one day transforming human relationships. It is a transformation which has as yet slight basis in reality.

Meanwhile, it seems as true as ever that women remain disadvantaged in marriage, despite more acceptance of the *idea* of sexual equality. Moreover, women themselves seem to know it. Another recent survey by Cowie and Lees of teenage girls in two comprehensive schools in London found that all the girls took it for granted that they would marry. But they were 'realistic', not romantic about it. They saw marriage as leading to domestic burdens, unequally shared, if at all. They reported the isolation, frustration and often violence experienced by their own mothers, who rarely went out, had few interests and felt undervalued: 'My Mum hates being at home . . .', '. . . they haven't got much to look forward to', and so on. Though the girls saw marriage as inevitable once they got older and wanted children, they wanted to have their fun first, certain that there would be little of it later: 'I think once you get married you lose pride in yourself, really', whereas the boys can 'still go around free'.[16]

Other features of women's lives today contribute to this depressing failure to improve women's lot generally. Sex segregation still confines women to a narrow selection of lower-paid, least-valued jobs. This means that women, who are now 40 per cent of the workforce, get only 25 per cent of the pay.[17] The problems of single parents and their children are largely a product of the lower wages paid for jobs which are seen as women's work, combined with inadequate child benefits and child-care provision. Research on one-parent children, for example, reveals that children of single mothers are neither more emotionally disturbed nor intellectually disadvantaged. The single significant factor in their lives is greater poverty.[18] Women who live alone or support unemployed or disabled husbands clearly also suffer a relative economic disadvantage.

One thing we need to examine at the moment is the effect of current Tory pro-family rhetoric and of Tory policies on the welfare of different family groupings, and of women generally. There is, of course, no necessary correlation between the adoption of a pro-family rhetoric and policies which might improve the position of family groupings. Nor even between such rhetoric and policies which might encourage, or perhaps force,

women back into full-time housework. Indeed, it is becoming
ever more clear, as a recent discussion bulletin on the family
concludes, that 'families are suffering more as a result of
government policies today than at any time since the war'.[19]
And more surprisingly perhaps, the ever-increasing financial
strain on parents is going to *increase* the pressure on women to
take on paid work, particularly women with children or other
dependants.

In meeting their promise to 'be vigilant to safeguard and
enhance the quality of family life', the Tory Party refers to two
things. They have sold off council housing so that families who
were previously publicly housed are now privately housed.
Meanwhile, the public housing stock overall has dropped drastically. They have provided public funds for a few children to
attend private schools. Meanwhile, they have made massive
cuts in public education, so that school meals have doubled in
price (on average) and parents must pay more for textbooks and
other educational materials.

What they do *not* refer to is far more considerable. Changes
in tax laws under the Tories have been to the detriment of
families with children compared to those without, while low-
paid parents pay proportionately more tax than parents with
high incomes. Child benefit has fallen since 1979, and is now
worth less in purchasing power than the combined value of
family allowance and child tax allowance in 1946. The value of
maternity benefits, already among the worst in Europe, was cut
by the Tories, together with cuts in the value of unemployment,
sickness and invalidity benefit. In addition, since 1980 it is
almost impossible for single parents to claim for clothes, shoes
or fuel.[20]

Capital expenditure on under-fives was planned to drop by
30 per cent in 1981, and current expenditure by 4 per cent.
Though variations between different local authorities in nursery
provision are wide, those who follow Tory policies provide few

or even no under-fives provision. Government spokesmen (*sic*) have stated that they have no intention of increasing under-fives provision. Boyson has reiterated that it is best for mothers of young children to be at home with them.[21] Personal social services for the elderly are now being cut, as local authorities have cut domiciliary services, home-help services, meals on wheels and day-care facilities to meet state-imposed spending cuts. This makes it harder, if not impossible, for families to care for elderly relatives at home. In short, with friends like Mrs Thatcher, who needs to 'smash the family'? Tory pro-family sentiments relate to pro-family policies (ones which might assist those caring for dependants) like the expression of love relates to the act of murder.

But is Thatcherism really convincing us all of its rationalization that a reduction in the state's commitment to welfare can restore the integrity of the family, and women's place of honour (the honour of sacrifice) within it? There is not much evidence that it is. Though Patrick Jenkin can assure us that, 'The family must be the front-line defence when Gran needs help', recent events like the huge support for the nurses' strike suggest that people *are* aware of the overwhelming importance of state welfare provision. All evidence suggest that the *less* the financial burden, the more likely relatives will, or can, care for the elderly and needy. Trades Union Congress policy on under-fives outlined in 1979 stated its support for comprehensive services on demand for all working parents of young children. And Doug Grieve of the Tobacco Workers' Union in 1981 demanded a reconstruction of the welfare system 'to be built upon new socialist principles', that is, rejecting the Beveridge idea that the woman's place is in the home.[22]

Indeed, Thatcherism itself, while immensely increasing the work-load and stress of women in the home – through increased poverty and cuts in services – remains ambivalent about women's rights. In this way it is unlike the pro-family movement in the United States, supported by Reaganism, which is directly anti-feminist – explicitly against abortion and equal rights for women, as well as anti-gay. The American New Right has now successfully undermined the equal rights legislation feminists had fought for, as well as attacking abortion rights and removing state funding for abortions. Its proposed Family Protection Act, supported by the tirelessly active Moral Majority and National Pro-Family Coalition, aims to strengthen parental authority and, in particular, paternal authority, while attacking legal funding for divorce, homosexual rights and abortion. In contrast, Britain's Thatcher government has an officially 'neutral' position on abortion, divorce and homosexual rights.

While it remains true that abortion facilities on the National Heath Service are inadequate, that there are delays of two or three weeks, and many doctors still display punitive attitudes to women seeking abortion, our current Minister of Health denies that there are any plans to restrict abortion services.[23] (This is despite the surreptitious removal of non-medical reasons for abortion on forms for surgeons in March 1981, which was successfully flouted by the gynaecologist Peter Huntingford and his colleague.) It seems likely that the Tories are more interested in promoting private abortion facilities in line with their general support for privatization of services. Nor have the main right-wing pressure groups, SPUC and LIFE, had any particular success lately, though we might expect Thatcherism to provide a suitable political terrain for them. In 1982, LIFE lost its prosecution of Dr Arthur for failing to preserve the life of a severely handicapped baby against the wishes of its parents, although it has managed to provide some funding for its anti-abortion services from the Department of the Environment, and has applied for further funding from the Department of Health and Social Security. But a recent survey of attitudes to abortion showed that 82 per cent of *both* Conservative and

Labour voters believed that choice as to whether to terminate a pregnancy should be left to the woman in consultation with her doctor, and surprisingly, that 75 per cent of Conservatives as against 69 per cent of Labour agreed with National Health Service provision for abortion.[24] Moreover, in a recent statement on divorce, Patrick Jenkin argued: 'We move on to difficult ground if we argue that government should take responsibility for, or even directly try to influence, how people live their lives.'[25]

It is true that Thatcherism has succeeded in mobilizing reactionary populist sentiments of patriotism, anti-trade unionism and anti-collectivism as the terrain of political debate has lurched defensively rightwards in this period of recession. But its pro-family rhetoric is less consistent – tempered by the continued success of feminism in mobilizing support for women's rights and equality. Moreover, despite frequent evocation of the importance of women's role in the family (a practice to which the Labour Party in the past was not averse, particularly when it was making cuts), there is little evidence that Thatcher's policies are having the effect of returning women to the home. They may well, though, be having the tragic effect of making it harder for women and children to leave violent homes, as public housing stock dries up (two thirds of the recent round of central government cuts have fallen on housing), legal aid is now denied for most matrimonial work, and enforced cuts on local authority budgets threaten Women's Aid refuges with closure. But obviously women's job opportunities are determined not by Tory rhetoric but in the economic environment of recession, industrial decline and restructuring, and deflationary policies. All of which have effects on women and family organization.

Under Thatcherism, job opportunities are supposed to be left to market forces, which has meant a disastrous increase in unemployment. Male unemployment rose from 6·7 per cent in

1979 to 15·4 per cent in mid 1982, while the female rate rose from 4·3 per cent to 9·1 per cent.[26] This does not take into account, among other things, the fact that more women than men do not bother to register (a 1977–8 survey estimated that 45 per cent of women compared to 24 per cent of men did not register).[27] But it would seem that the differential effects on men and women in the job market, where manufacturing jobs have declined faster than service jobs and where the effects of new technologies are unclear, mean that women are not any longer necessarily going to lose jobs faster than men. For instance, in Wales it is predicted that, in the coming decade, women will outnumber men in paid work, as a result of changes in employment patterns.[28] Moreover, the expansion of part-time and 'job-splitting' opportunities, which the government has decided to encourage, should make it possible for women to do paid work as well as onerous domestic workloads. This suits many employers, as women part-time workers are the most highly exploited. On top of missing out on various workers' rights, their average hourly earnings in April 1981 were only 58 per cent of those for full-time male workers.[29]

Ironically, an expansion of part-time work opportunities – for both women and men, and at adequate rates – to enable the sharing of domestic chores and pleasures has been put forward by some as an element of socialist feminist policy.[30] Clearly this government's intentions are far from wishing to provide possibilities for greater choice and sharing between men and women in the home. Nor, in general, have they. Today women in employment, for instance, are likely to fear leaving their jobs to have children, because of the fear of future permanent unemployment. Other women, and in particular very young women who can find no jobs, may feel forced into motherhood as the only role available to them. For instance, with no other identification with an adult role, it is not surprising to hear teenage mothers say, as I heard in a recent television programme on teenage pregnancy: 'You feel a lot older if you've got a bubbie, people don't look down on you like if you're unemployed.' Having a baby can give unemployed young women a reason for living, though supporting yourself and your baby on a single parent's allowance of about £30 a week will not make for much good living, for either of them.

Again, the 1980 Employment Act means employers can more easily refuse a woman her job back after maternity leave, which also threatens women's choices on whether to have children, as well as how they should be cared for. Family poverty, if nothing else, will keep women in employed work. But the overall unemployment rate, and the threat of unemployment experienced by men and women, combined with a declining standard of living for nearly all workers under Thatcherism, can only increase tension, stress and crisis in the family lives of all but the highly paid. Feminists have perhaps too readily accepted the rhetoric of Thatcherism, believing that women will be – or could be – forced back into the home. The reality remains more contradictory. This means that any demand for a 'woman's right to work' must always encompass a more subtle understanding of women's disadvantages both at home and at work, where the demands of the workplace ignore the demands of home.

So there is little to suggest that women will be forced back into the home; though some who may wish to stay home will be forced out to work, while others who wish to go out to work will be forced to stay home. But employed women's domestic 'duties', on top of their paid work, *will* continue to become ever more burdensome. This means that domestic tensions between men and women will continue, and along with them the *potential* to challenge the gender division in the family which underpins women's inequality both in the home and outside it. For it is women's employment, together with accessible fertility control, which has both created the possibility for women's independence and at the same time brought into the open women's inequality as badly paid workers and as overburdened house-wives. We should not simply accuse the Thatcher government of undermining the family by increasing family poverty and tension, though it is. But we should also see that now is the time to stress as central to Left politics, socialist feminist strategies which could both create real choices as to how we live, work and support each other, and also, at least for women, improve the quality of both our domestic and our 'working' lives.

It was precisely the hypocrisy of assumptions of domestic bliss that were so perceptively laid bare in the more radical politics generated by the prosperity of the 1960s. All recent surveys reveal that the majority of women do not like full-time housework and would like better child-care facilities. For ex-ample, a Gallup Poll commissioned by *Woman's Own* in 1979 of a representative sample of 4,000, found that four out of five mothers would want to go out to work, whether or not financial pressure drove them, and that 96 per cent thought that the council should provide child-care provision. But half of their sample had been unable to work, while more than one in three mothers of under-fives who had jobs were forced into punishing evening and night shifts. The myth is that women feel happy and fulfilled under current arrangements for motherhood and housework. The reality is that they do not.

People who live alone, in particular, suffer from the lack of adequate community and welfare facilities, though nearly all of us, young or old and however we live, also suffer in different ways from inadequate welfare provision. Indeed, the gulf we feel between our public and private lives, and the typical lack of any wider community ties which can bridge our experience of that gulf, impoverishes all our lives; whether we live alone or with others. The traditional ideal of 'family', with its strictly private provision for personal and social needs, so beloved by the Right, is one which denies the importance of more social community provision for needs. It is one which isolates family members as much as it mediates against any more collective or communal responsibility for others.

A socialist feminist perspective would seek to foster new and wider bonds of love and loyalty beyond ties of blood and marriage. We want neither to push all women into the labour market nor to return them to what never were the joys of solitary motherhood and housework, but, through shorter 'working' hours, to integrate work and family life in ways that would enrich them both. We want neither to prescribe nor prevent traditional family arrangements, but to increase the possibility for choice and equality in our domestic lives (though we are totally opposed to the legal terms of marriage which define women as dependent). We want benefits and policies which provide a genuine supportive framework in which we can go about raising our children and caring for dependent people. We want to give value to the sorts of work women have always done. But we want to do it differently, in ways that allow a greater choice for both men and women. Feminists want a society where there is real equality between women and men, where both can and must assume greater control over domestic life and support for those in need of care.

All this means the Left raising feminist perspectives on many fronts. In the traditional Labour Movement, it means fighting for state policies which improve welfare services generally, increasing child benefit and allowances to cover the real cost of caring for children and other dependants, while recognizing women as independent persons, both sexually and economically. It means trade unions fighting for shorter working hours, the opening of new jobs and training to women, and discarding notions of the male 'family wage'. And as feminists we know it means continual confrontation with men to push them to take responsibility for children and all those in need of care and support. We know also that we can rely on neither the trade union movement nor any government to remove the hierarchies which have throughout history oppressed women and all those more vulnerable in society. The struggle for new social priorities which link our working and domestic lives will be fought both in traditional political forums and also in the streets and elsewhere by women challenging and confronting male power, and demanding that men confront each other.

Both the women's movement and the New Left sought sexual liberation and change in personal life as part of their emphasis on personal creativity and wellbeing. Their success was based on this. We must hold on to the importance of that struggle, even if our optimism has been tempered by the inevitable tension between women and men, heterosexual and gay people, as we challenged the sexist structures which have shaped all our personal histories. But whether we like it or whether we don't, family life will continue to change. The sooner we recognize and support the potential for sexual equality created by that change, the greater the chance of unity between socialists and feminists fighting to improve our lives. Current government policies exacerbate the pressure on families. But that pressure will not now disappear by calling for a return to the *traditional* family, kept stable through the wife's inescapable dependence. To call for the return of the traditional family is like calling for the return of the British Empire. Its time has passed.

Notes and References

1. F. Mount, *The Subversive Family*, Jonathan Cape, London, 1982.
2. M. Thatcher, *Women in a Changing World*, Press Office, Downing Street, London, 1982.
3. ibid., p. 34.
4. M. Piercy, *Braided Lives*, Allen Lane, Harmondsworth, 1982, p. 8.
5. ibid., p. 108.
6. J. Bernard, *The Future of Marriage*, Penguin Books, Harmondsworth, 1976.
7. See A. Oakley, *Subject Women*, Martin Robertson, Oxford, 1981.
8. A. Cherlin, *Marriage Divorce Remarriage*, Harvard University Press, 1982.

9. *Annual Abstract of Statistics*, CSO, London, 1982, Table 3.71.

10. C. Rossiter and M. Wick, *Crisis or Challenge? Family Care, Elderly People and Social Policy*, Study Commission on the Family, London, p. 13.

11. ibid., p. 67.

12. ibid., p. 26.

13. P. Mansfield, 'With Stars in Their Eyes and a Wife at the Sink', *Guardian*, 9 February 1982.

14. Oakley, *Subject Women*, pp. 250, 251.

15. B. Friedan, *The Second Stage*, Michael Joseph, London, 1982.

16. C. Cowie and S. Lees, 'Slags or Drags', *Feminist Review*, autumn 1981, p. 23.

17. H. Neuberger in the *Guardian*, 21 August 1982.

18. N. Smelser, 'The Disappearing Parents', *New Society*, 5 August 1982, p. 215.

19. J. Coussins and A. Coote, *The Family in the Firing Line. A Discussion Document on Family Policy*, Poverty Pamphlet, NCCL/CPAG, March 1981, p. 6.

20. ibid.

21. *Hansard*, House of Commons, 27 October 1981.

22. D. Grieve, 'Family Policy', in *Poverty*, 50, December 1981.

23. See *National Abortion Campaign Newsletter*, August 1982.

24. C. Francome, *Gallup on Abortion*, Middlesex Polytechnic, 1982.

25. P. Jenkin, Foreword to *The Future of Marriage*, Conservative Political Centre, London, 1982, pp. 5–6.

26. *Employment Gazette*, Department of Employment, July 1982.

27. Quoted in *Labour Research*, March 1982, p. 61.

28. G. Williams, 'Land of Our Fathers', in *Marxism Today*, August 1982, p. 24.

29. ibid., p. 23.

30. J. Gardiner and S. Smith, 'Feminism and the Alternative Economic Strategy', *Socialist Economic Review*, 1982.

Index

MORE ABOUT PENGUINS
AND PELICANS

For further information about books available from Penguins please write to Dept EP, Penguin Books Ltd, Harmondsworth, Middlesex UB7 ODA.

In the U.S.A.: For a complete list of books available from Penguins in the United States write to Dept DG, Penguin Books, 299 Murray Hill Parkway, East Rutherford, New Jersey 07073.

In Canada: For a complete list of books available from Penguins in Canada write to Penguin Books Canada Ltd, 2801 John Street, Markham, Ontario L3R 1B4.

In Australia: For a complete list of books available from Penguins in Australia write to the Marketing Department, Penguin Books Australia Ltd, P.O. Box 257, Ringwood, Victoria 3134.

In New Zealand: For a complete list of books available from Penguins in New Zealand write to the Marketing Department, Penguin Books (N.Z.) Ltd, P.O. Box 4019, Auckland 10.